D0613599

Good Seeds

Whenever the Menomini enter a region, the wild rice spreads ahead; whenever they leave it the wild rice passes. (Elder, quoted in Keesing, 1939)

Good Seeds

A Menominee Indian Food Memoir

Thomas Pecore Weso

WISCONSIN HISTORICAL SOCIETY PRESS

Published by the Wisconsin Historical Society Press
Publishers since 1855

The Wisconsin Historical Society helps people connect to the past by collecting, preserving, and sharing stories. Founded in 1846, the Society is one of the nation's finest historical institutions.

wisconsin**history**.org

Order books by phone toll free: (888) 999-1669 • *Order books online:* shop.wisconsinhistory.org
Join the Wisconsin Historical Society: wisconsinhistory.org/membership

© 2016 by Thomas Pecore Weso

The following pieces first appeared in a slightly different format in the following:

"Fire: Grandmother's Morning," in *Native Literatures: Generations* 1, no. 3 (Fall 2010), www.nai.msu.edu/publication/native _literatures_generations.

"Prayer: Grandfather's Dreaming," in *The Muckleshoot Review* 3 (2011): 70–74.

"Partridges" excerpt and "Greens" excerpt published in Heid Erdrich's *Original Local: Indigenous Foods, Stories, and Recipes from the Upper Midwest* (St. Paul: Minnesota Historical Society Press, 2013).

"German Beer," first published as "Death on the Reservation" in *Show + Tell: A Celebration of Art, an Expression of Word* (Kansas City, MO: Potpourri and Kansas City Artists Coalition): 141–143. Reprinted in *Yellow Medicine Review* (Spring 2011): 44–50.

For permission to reuse material from *Good Seeds* (ISBN 978-0-87020-771-6; e-book ISBN 978-0-87020-772-3), please access www.copy right.com or contact the Copyright Clearance Center, Inc. (CCC), 222 Rosewood Drive, Danvers, MA 01923, 978-750-8400. CCC is a not-for-profit organization that provides licenses and registration for a variety of users.

Many of the recipes in this book call for ingredients that were traditionally used as food. However, proper identification and preparation of these ingredients is the responsibility of the reader. Neither the author nor the publisher shall be responsible for any loss, injury, or damage resulting from information included here.

Printed in Canada
Designed by Percolator Graphic Design

20 19 18 17 16   1 2 3 4 5

Library of Congress Cataloging-in-Publication Data applied for.

♾ The paper used in this publication meets the minimum requirements of the American National Standard for Information Sciences—Permanence of Paper for Printed Library Materials, ANSI Z39.48-1992.

To my wife, Denise,
and to our children, PEmecewan, Daniel, David, and Diane

In the back row, from left, are my mother, Frances (Weso) Walker; my grandmother Jennie (Heath) Weso; my aunt Lorraine (Weso) Smith; and my grandfather Moon Weso. In the front row, my older brother Gerald stands on the left and I am on the right. FROM THE AUTHOR'S COLLECTION

Contents

Preface

My Grandfather Moon was considered a medicine man. His morning prayers were the foundation for each day's meals. This is how I understand cooking, as part of a family process that includes spirit, the forest environment, and fuel for cooking—all before the meal can be prepared. In the kitchen, my grandmother Jennie "made fire" in a traditional way every morning before dawn in a wood-burning stove. She woke her sons to go out hunting or fishing, depending on the season. As I grew up, my uncles taught me to hunt bear, deer, squirrels, raccoons, and even skunks for the daily larder. Grandma oversaw huge breakfasts of wild game, fish, and fruit pies. She organized her daughters into effective teams for both meals and the family business of food stands.

Grandmother Jane (Heath) Weso, known as Jennie, lived from 1911 to 1979, and Grandfather Monroe Weso, known as Kaso (Moon), lived from 1904 to 1983. They attended assimilationist boarding schools where they learned about the dietary culture of the larger United States. Their lives spanned the early-twentieth-century development of the logging industry, termination of the Menominee Tribe in 1958, and restoration of the tribe in 1973. They saw the rise of legal, religious, and educational rights for Native peoples. Six children, many grandchildren, and several generations of great-grandchildren descend directly from this couple.

The culinary experience of my grandparents' large household left vivid memories. I remember the excitement of "sugar bush," maple sugar gatherings that included dances as well as hard work. I remember our family's food stand at the Menominee County Fair and yearly powwow, where my grandmother's meat pies and baked beans were a favorite.

My grandparents shared many foods with their northern Wisconsin European settler neighbors. They also perpetuated ancient hunting, gathering, farming, and storage practices from the earliest Algonquin woodland dwellers. Jennie and Moon Weso were an important link to the food knowledge of the earliest times. They also modeled an integral aspect of Indigenous survival—adaptation to new conditions. The most basic element of survival is food, and the open attitude toward all kinds of food has been an important asset for the Menominee people.

Following my family tradition, I attended Haskell Indian Nations University, where my grandfather attended in the 1910s and then my mother, aunts, and uncles attended in the 1940s and 1950s. My daughter received a degree from Haskell also. In 1994 I received an associate of arts degree, and from there I continued my education at the University of Kansas. I received both an undergraduate degree in anthropology and a master's degree in global Indigenous nations studies. By then, I had married a Kansan and settled in the river town of Lawrence, less than an hour from Kansas City. Mild winters are a luxury, and hot, dry summers are a penance. In Lawrence, I learned the rich food traditions of the lower Midwest, including barbeque, comfort food, Southwest spices, and bison. Cooking interests me, especially the cultural context for food usage. As I told stories about Menominee cooking to my wife, she encouraged me to write them down. This book is the result of several years of stories, added gradually. My wife, Denise Low, is a writer and helped me with editing suggestions and organization.

My appreciation goes to all my family who helped with this book with encouragement and many great meals. Thank you to Frances (Weso) Walker, Bobby and Nita (Weso) Perez, Mary Walker-Sanapaw, Donovan Walker, Terri Katchenago, Gerald Weso, Morgan Buttner, Laura Paredes, Rachel Corn, Yvonne

Katchenago, and Monroe Weso. Aunt Nita Perez's help with newspaper archives is also appreciated.

As I pass sixty years of age, I appreciate more fully the strength of the generations before me. I hope this collection helps to preserve the rich food culture of the Menominees and of all Indigenous peoples. My grandparents were important figures throughout my life. This book is an attempt to explain their legacy.

Fire: Grandmother's Morning

The Menomini wife is allowed a rather wide latitude of choice in her activities. She may leave her children with a grand-mother and accompany her husband on fishing and hunting trips and help him with housebuilding and the gathering of ferns, or she may choose to remain close to her home and chil-dren, performing the more conventional tasks of child-care, cooking, tanning, washing clothes, and sewing. (Louise S. Spindler, "Menomini Women and Culture Change," 1962)

If I were not farming, I should make mats and quilts and beadwork, and I should go to Neopit to do washing, so as to earn money. I should sell all the mats. Baskets too I should make. When I had made a great quantity, I should sell them all. From this I should obtain much money. . . . I should al-ways gather raspberries and sell them. That is what I should do, if I did not farm. ("How a Menomini Woman Earns Money" Maskwawanahkwatok, in Bloomfield, Menominee Texts, 1928)

My grandmother was the one who made fire every morning. She always used that term, "making fire," even after they had modern conveniences on the Menominee Indian reservation in northern Wisconsin. Later, setting the thermostat was also "making fire." But when I was really young, we had a wood stove, and getting up to make fire was literally getting up to ignite kindling and wood.

Their house also had a small propane wall heater in the kitchen, with open flames—a true safety hazard, but it helped keep alive the tradition of fire and fire keepers.

Safe or not, Grandma got up early, four a.m. First she started the stove, preparing for the first meal of the day. When the kindling flamed inside the tiny mica window, she put a pot of coffee on the back burner, where it would simmer the rest of the day.

Making fire also meant starting the big boiler. Since our grandfather was the justice of the peace, game warden, and government officer on the rez, we had government housing, but with a twist. The roomy old house in Keshena, Wisconsin, had once been the Indian Service jail. Our bedrooms had been cells, and the kitchen had been in the office area. The boiler was in a dungeon-like basement. Even though it might still have embers left over from the night before, it needed to be freshly stoked to counter the northern cold. I can remember it being very cold when I was young, colder than it is today with global warming. Diesel fuel starts to gel at forty below zero. Pine trees start to burst at twenty below, from the sap freezing. So this was the kind of cold we faced, and making fire in that dark, gloomy basement was survival. Stoking the stove, furnace, and heater—in that order— began the process of day.

After the household fires were made, Grandma dressed and poured herself black coffee. To combat the chill, everybody, even the kids, drank coffee. It was the brand with the logo of a man wearing a turban, Hills Brothers. Menominee men wore turbans through the nineteenth century and into the first part of the twentieth century, so Hills Brothers seemed a tad Menominee. The Menominee term for *coffee* is a borrowed word, *ko-peh*, and it is a word everybody knows. We put lots of evaporated sweetened milk into the coffee, so for kids this was a source of calcium.

Coffee also was a part of my grandfather's extensive politicking, which began at daybreak. The old Indians went to bed when it was dark and got out and around when it was light, so we could expect company starting at daybreak. So another reason for the big coffeepot was politics. Many visitors were relatives from the Mole Lake Ojibwe and the Forest County Potawatomi who were heavily into the old religion, which also was considered to be black magic. They were spooky, and no one wanted to offend them. Hospitality was important for survival in many ways, and we always wanted to have food and drink to offer them. Coffee was ready any time the sun was up, and freshness was not necessary.

Who sat at the breakfast table was complicated. Grandma had many, many relatives by blood, marriage, or other circumstances. I knew them as uncles and aunts, but I could not begin to estimate which were honorary and which were blood kin. My cousins and I and other relatives were often at the table every day for weeks and months at a time. Also, we had people who worked for us. Meals—morning and evening—often fed two dozen people. My grandmother started the fire not just for the immediate family, but also for the extended group that would congregate throughout the day.

My grandmother was queen of the house. Menominees are known as matriarchal since our clans go through the mother's family. Women also have political power in certain spheres. Grandma would overrule my grandfather on any number of occasions, usually having to do with family or household affairs. In the old days, the clan mother made decisions about who ate and who did not, which meant, during famine seasons, that she held the supreme authority over life and death. This is the ultimate political role. My grandfather usually made decisions outside the house, but even there, if family members were involved, she had the power to overrule him. Within the household, no question, she was the supreme authority. But no decision was made in haste. Many negotiations went on while coal-black *ko-peh* poured into people's cups.

Breakfast depended on what time of the year it was and who was home. For example, my uncle Bobby was the best fisherman in the family. During warm weather, Grandma would wake him at four a.m. to go fishing for trout. In the fall, she would get him up to go spear northern pikes as they migrated. He would stand on a certain big rock, and that was a sight. I didn't like bass, so Bobby had to catch other fish especially for me. He was such a good fisherman that he could go out the door at four a.m. and bring back fish at five. Grandma or my aunts cleaned them and had them floured and in the pan frying for breakfast by six.

In late summer, Uncle Billy, who was the best shot at squirrels and partridges, would get up and go hunting for small game. The animals were plumper because of late-summer fat accumulation. Uncle Buddy and Uncle Donny were also good hunters, but they were better at hunting larger game, deer and bear. So it depended what season it was. Grandma would awaken different family hunters to get food. Whatever any of us brought back was our breakfast or dinner. I developed good aim and could get squirrels with one shot. We did not waste ammunition. If no squirrels were about, then rabbits, raccoons, porcupines, beavers, or any other small creature would do.

For breakfast, we also ate bacon and eggs, dishes borrowed from European neighbors. Grandpa liked to have a wide variety of foods at any meal. His ideal was to have a spoonful of twenty different foods at a meal, like a Thanksgiving feast. My uncle once told me that Menominee people were strong and had better resistance to diseases than some other groups because they were able to prepare so many different foods. Some tribes depended on one primary food source, like bison or shellfish. Menominees had almost no food taboos and knew how to hunt, fish, farm, and gather a wide variety of plants and animals. So we had bacon and eggs, along with the fish or game caught that morning.

We seldom ate oatmeal. It might be a good, hot meal in the cold, but we did not have the custom of eating it. We preferred cornmeal as a hot cereal—boiled in water until it thickened. My mother started eating oatmeal at boarding school in Kansas, at Haskell Institute, so on occasion, in deference to her, breakfast included oatmeal. It was served Menominee style, on a plate with salt, pepper, and butter. It was never sweetened or served with milk, cinnamon, or raisins. In the same way, we did not eat pancakes until Aunt Nita attended boarding school and acquired a taste for them—and most of these, served to other family members, ended up as the dog's meal.

We had potatoes at every meal and cornbread several times a day. We had venison at least once a day, often at breakfast. My grandfather always had a store of canned and dried venison, survival food. My uncles provided fresh deer meat in the fall and early winter. I never understood that venison could taste good until after I left the reservation. Menominee County deer were so wary of hunters that they ran off their fat. I thought all venison was tough and stringy.

We usually ate cottage cheese for breakfast. This seems incongruous for Indigenous peoples, but that was another staple, like coffee. There was a small dairy in Gresham, a nearby town, and they delivered to the rez. Their delivery man was on the same route for over sixty years, well into his seventies. He traveled daily to the Menominee, Polish, and German communities. He was a phantom figure because he delivered milk before I woke, no matter how cold the weather. My first job was at the Gresham school cafeteria, washing dishes, and there I finally met the man. I was fourteen, and his delivery schedule was later in the day for the school. He used to flirt with those old cafeteria cook ladies, which amused me greatly. I passed this tidbit on to my family, and we enjoyed this story at breakfast, as we finally learned more about this phantom. The milkman also brought milk, but we didn't drink much milk. We used canned sweetened evaporated milk for coffee.

My grandmother often had preserved fruit pies for breakfast as well—apple, blackberry, blueberry, or gooseberry. Looking back, it is hard for me to imagine how she had all this food cooking on one stove—pies, bacon and eggs, fish and game, dried venison, cornbread, potatoes, and more. The morning meal was heated through with the day's first fire, and dinner was kept warm by the last ember-fueled heat.

What I realize now is the influence of Catholicism on my family's eating patterns. My grandmother learned how to cook from the Catholics. When my grandmother was young, they made her attend Catholic boarding school, which was the public school at the time. My grandfather never went. He practiced the traditional Menominee religion and then the Native American Church. My grandpa hated Catholics because they stole the children to go to school away from home. Grandpa had equal dislike for Lutherans, who had a boarding school in Wittenberg for the western side of the rez. Our option as children was to go to school with the Lutherans or the Catholics, or to go away to Haskell Institute in Kansas. At Haskell they didn't care what your religion was, as long as you were there for head count at morning muster. Many of my relatives went to Kansas to avoid religion.

But Grandma attended the local Catholic boarding school as a child—St. Joe's in Keshena—and learned white people's cooking. For lunch, she fixed my grandfather his favorite sandwiches to carry with him: bologna with Miracle Whip on white bread. So the influence of boarding school cooking came into the family—oatmeal, pancakes, bread, canned milk, and preserved lunchmeats.

My grandmother never threw away any food. If, after many, many meals, a bit of leftovers remained, Rocky, the dog, got it.

He was a mutt, Uncle Buddy's great big bird dog. He was black and white and had long hair. He used to go out and fight with all the other dogs and win. He never bit people, but he harmed so many other dogs that he was considered a public danger. The sheriff came over several times to shoot him, but someone in the family would throw themselves between the dog and the sheriff. After many reprieves and table scraps, he finally died of old age. He is buried along the Wolf River, along with other family members. Rocky benefited from the bounty of Grandma, and he played his part in our meals, even though he was not seated at the table.

So fire started the day. It meant survival from cold and hunger, for Grandma and Grandpa and all their children, grandchildren, cousins, in-laws, adopted relatives, and even the dog. At six a.m., every day, a hot breakfast was on the table. That was also the time that Grandma put on her coat and left for work. She worked sometimes as a nurse, and other times she ran a store across the highway. All those years, I never saw her sit down and eat a meal in peace.

Oatmeal, Menominee Style

⅛ teaspoon salt
1¼ cups oatmeal
2 teaspoons bacon grease or fresh butter
Salt and pepper, to taste

Bring 2 cups of water to boil. Add salt. Stir in oatmeal, reduce heat, and let simmer 10 minutes, stirring occasionally to keep it from sticking. Serve on a plate with a teaspoon of bacon grease or a pat of butter, with salt and pepper to taste.

Pan-Fried Trout

6 whole trout, cleaned (other panfish can be substituted:
    bass, perch, walleye)
1½ teaspoons salt
½ cup flour or cornmeal
1 teaspoon paprika
½ teaspoon pepper
2 cups oil

Wash fish thoroughly and dry. Salt well. Combine the flour or cornmeal, paprika, and pepper and mix well. Roll the fish in the flour mixture, knocking off excess. Add oil to a large, shallow pan, and fry fish about 5 minutes, then turn. Fry another 3 minutes, just until just crisp and golden. Do not overcook.

Fried Squirrels

5–7 squirrels, washed thoroughly and cleaned
1 tablespoon salt
3–4 peeled, whole onions
¾ cup oil, lard, or shortening

Parboil the squirrels, salt, and onions in a kettle of boiling water. Remove from heat when the meat is fork tender. Remove squirrels and onions and drain. Pat the squirrels dry. Heat a large skillet on high. Add oil and lower the heat slightly. When the oil is heated through, add the squirrels and onions. Cook until brown and crisp.

Fruit Pie

2 cups plus 1 tablespoon flour, divided, plus extra for rolling
    the crust
1 teaspoon salt
⅔ cup shortening or lard
⅓ cup ice water
3 cups apples, cherries, or blueberries (canned or fresh)
2 tablespoons sugar
1 tablespoon butter, chopped into small pieces

To make the crust: In a mixing bowl, stir together 2 cups sifted flour and salt. Add shortening or lard (half can be butter, for a richer pie crust). Chop the shortening into the flour with a pastry blender (or two knives) until the mixture is cut into pea-sized bits. Sprinkle the ice water into the mixture gradually, stirring with a fork until just enough water has been added to allow the dough to hold together. Form the dough into a ball, handling it as little as possible. Wrap the ball in wax paper and chill.

To make the filling: Drain fruit, reserving ½ cup juice. Place fruit in a mixing bowl. In a small bowl, mix reserved juice with sugar and 1 tablespoon flour or other thickener. Pour over the fruit. (If using fresh fruit, simply toss the fruit with the sugar and flour before filling crust.)

When shortening has hardened, roll into two ⅛-inch-thick rounds on a board lightly dusted with flour, one round slightly larger than the other (the larger one will be the bottom crust). Transfer the larger crust to a pie pan, then add filling. Dot filling with butter pieces and cover with the second crust. Cut several slits or designs near the center to let out steam. Bake at 350°F for 45 minutes, or until brown on top.

Prayer: Grandfather's Dreaming

Grasshopper and the Origin of Tobacco—One day Manabush was walking past a high mountain when he smelled a
delightful fragrance. . . . The mountain was home to a Giant
who was known to be the keeper of tobacco. Manabush found
a cavern in the side of the mountain and went inside, following a passage which led into the center of the mountain where
the Giant lived . . . [and he asked] for some tobacco. The
Giant told [him] . . . to come back in a year. Manabush . . .
looked around the Giant's cavern and saw bags and bags of
tobacco. . . . So he snatched one, dashed [up] the mountain,
closely pursued by the Giant. When Manabush reached the
edge of a cliff, he fell down flat and the Giant leaped over him
and fell over the cliff and into the chasm. Manabush grabbed
the Giant by the back and threw him to the ground and
said, "For your stinginess, you will become the Grasshopper,
and everyone will know you by your stained mouth. You will
become a pest and bother all those who raise tobacco." Then
Manabush took the tobacco home and divided it among the
people and gave them the seed so they could grow it themselves and use it for offerings and blessings. (Hoffman, 1890)

My grandmother always got up at four in the morning, every
morning, and started the household fires. My grandfather, however, emerged from his bedroom at six a.m., fully dressed and
groomed. He would come downstairs, and breakfast would be

waiting on the table for him. At the time I thought my grand-father slept until six, but I was wrong. I now believe that in the two hours between four and six, my grandfather would perform a ceremony and pray in private. I don't think even my grandmother knew exactly what he did. Among northern Indians, especially Menominees, men are expected to dream, and everything else is secondary. *Dreaming* is a word that suggests matters that are primarily spiritual. Grandpa's prayers were behind and within all our meals, even though we never participated in these morning devotions with him. This was an important, intangible part of all our meals. *Kinnikinnick,* or smoking herbs like tobacco, were essential to these unseen ceremonies.

Grandpa was one of the last of the old Indians, from that era before substantial intermingling of cultures. In those days Indi-ans stayed with Indians, and there weren't many outsiders on the reservation. He spoke his native language fluently. He was, nonetheless, as a Haskell graduate, a cultural go-between. In his public persona outside the reservation, he was a very refined man, like a Southern gentleman, genteel and charming. My grand-father could out–white man the white man in civility. That is the man I grew up with, as I accompanied him in his travels around northern Wisconsin. There were a few times when we were with other northern Indian bands—nearby Potawatomi, Ojibwe, and Ho-Chunk—and he allowed his Indian side to come through. But mostly he was a public leader among whites.

My grandfather expressed his private, Indian self in Peyote meetings, now known as the Native American Church. I went to Peyote meetings with my grandfather all my life until he died, and I saw that Indian side of him, but I always thought that was simply proper Native American Church behavior, not distinctive Indian culture. In Peyote meetings, I saw that he had visions and spoke in tongues. I learned how the cactus button from Texas and Mexico was another kind of food for our family. It is a complex plant with many properties known to heal body, mind, and spirit.

The Native American Church is autonomous from place to place. The Catholic church has regular rituals, so if one priest died, another would replicate the same ritual. Tipi meetings were ceremonies adapted to the occasion and with variance from person to person. This individuality was what I thought of as my grandpa's Menominee spiritual expression.

When I was thirty-five, I saw my grandfather wearing an Indian headband for the first time, in a Peyote meeting. This was during President Lyndon Johnson's Great Society, the era when people were expressing their cultural heritage more readily. Headbands had become a common thing. Anyone with one recessive Indian gene wore a headband. Those were the days when I always had a pair of moccasins. From early spring to late fall, I wore only moccasins, not as an expression of culture, but because they were very comfortable. At that time, I would not be teased or harassed.

So for the first time, in the 1960s, I saw my grandfather wearing a headband, colored in reds and blues on a field of yellow. Knowing a little something of the Algonquin motifs, I knew it was floral in the Great Lakes style, but it was not like anything I had seen before, nor have I seen it since. I don't know who made it for him. This was a gift from outside the family. My stepfather, a German American, was very good at duplicating patterns, and many Indian people bought things from him, but his designs were simpler. The beads on Grandpa's headband were very small and the design was very intricate, so I know it was not my stepfather's work.

Beading is a technical skill, with traditions like the peyote stitch, which my grandfather taught me to do. This stitch is like darning, with a couple of knots and then a bead and so forth, very time-consuming. This headband was not peyote stitch, but it had that intricacy. It is possible it was not made on a loom. It looked like each tiny, tiny bead was sewn onto something in isolation, so that the entire design was not evident until it was all done. Most designs made in the last hundred years are symmetrical, made in a binary pattern, and so with ten columns of beads there is a regularity and repetition. The headband design my grandfather was wearing did not have that regularity. It was free-flowing, and yet it was an evenly edged headband strip. I have not seen examples of this kind of artifact in all the museums I have been to, not even the earliest objects from the 1700s. This headband must have been made prior to then, just after contact with European traders, because it was made of glass beads. The gift of the headband indicates the esteem in which my grandfather was held among his people.

The small villages, isolated in the northwoods, consisted of people who were mostly related to each other. The Potawatomi tribe is one entity in that area, the Forest Band, and they include many Wesos or Weshos. Some Wesos migrated to live with the Prairie Band Potawatomis in Kansas. By circumstance, my grandfather, although Potawatomi, became enrolled in the Menominee tribe. Among these bands, my grandfather was what white people would call a medicine man. My grandfather's duty as a medicine man was to create a spiritual climate in which his relatives could survive and even thrive. This was his primary contribution to the family and community—spiritual sustenance. It was as important as food on the kitchen table.

A lot of people knew my grandfather. He got around as a game warden. Although he did not hunt or fish, he knew all the Menominee and Forest Band Potawatomi hunters and fishermen. He knew all the white storekeepers and officials in nearby Shawano, Wisconsin. My grandfather went out every day politicking, getting around and glad-handing both communities. He was not prejudiced, but he observed that the nature of white men was greed. He gave many examples, and I lived and watched, and he was right. If we'd continued sniping at each other, nobody would have survived, and it would have been all white people or all Indians, and because of numbers, probably the white people would have prevailed.

He carried news between factions and negotiated differences. I can now see that Grandpa was trying to create a political climate in accordance with a spiritual climate, and I think people expected him to do this in his role as a medicine man. My grandfather talked to white people, black people, Indian people, and he tried to learn how to interact with each equally. He never used the "N" word, and this was at a time when a lot of Menominees were going back and forth to Chicago and many came back with that word. My grandfather never told boastful stories about himself, as he was very modest, but he was a leader.

In the eighty-one years that my grandfather was on earth, he was in a Catholic church only one time, for a couple of hours, and he was already dead, so he didn't have much say in the matter. He did all of his spirituality outside the structures of organized religion. The essence of his spirituality was individuality. I suspect that my grandfather thought that churches in America are social structures seeking to modify behaviors. And those behaviors are legal and social in nature, not spiritual. In his view, churches prevent a person from being an individual. Little original thought occurs in churches. For the last hundred years or so, there has been a handbook of behaviors, a catechism, but people have to put their faith in the authors of the book. My grandfather put his faith in his experiences and heritage. He was on the trail of the essence of spirituality, that which guides all people. Perhaps he was able to discern some mode of thought that was used by many people. Grandpa was an independent seeker who looked for patterns in nature, in human behavior, and in spiritual practice.

Medicine men and women, and all people who are spiritual in that sense, practice at a local level, and if something doesn't work out, they find out about it fast. I don't think my grandfather would have given the advice to anybody that if you are a good person and obey the law and get persecuted, you turn the other cheek. This depends on the idea of heaven—after eighty years your reward is that you die and go to heaven. That kind of advice does not work in the practical world. He would have told you something more realistic: move, get another job, and go to school.

I think when my grandfather was praying, he was praying not to what white people call God or to the Great Mystery—but to something more elemental, perhaps nature. He knew plants, he knew herbs, he knew animals. The Great Mystery is a way for Indians to affirm what white people call God. Reciprocation defined his outlook, because if people abuse nature, they should not expect nature to provide food for the table. People are not at the apex of the food chain. Rather, all living creatures are an expression of God. We have the ability to kill, but we are not in control. We live among other living beings. I don't think he would have thought favorably of factory farming, not because he was afraid of wringing a few chickens' necks to feed the family, but because if an animal has to die, there should be some dignity to that death.

If the world is going to hell, it is because there is an imbalance of spirituality. If people feel good about themselves, they take better care of themselves, their domain, their town, and their land. So if a man like my grandfather wants to make a difference, he shows how people can feel better about themselves. That betterment has to be self-evident, or they won't continue it. This improves spiritual outlook as well. Part of Grandpa's teaching was gardening. We always had a family garden. If any of us went to the garden to do some watering or hoeing, we could see our efforts bear fruit. That reward also had a spiritual aspect.

People talk about the good old days, when things were simpler. But the old life was not simple. People had to order their day according to what nature was doing, not human desires. If it was the season to pick cranberries, my grandmother went out to the bogs and picked cranberries. It was a cool-season crop, when a film of ice was on the swamps. She could not wait for a warm day. She had to get out when the cranberries were ripe. The land had its ceremonies, unfolding through the seasons, and people followed them.

Our meals were not far removed from the woods or the lake or the garden. We could not decide, "Today pork would taste good." Those choices were planned a year ahead of time. If my grandfather wanted pork for his family, that meant he bought a pig and raised it until it was ready to butcher. The foundation for all these spiritual practices—easing relations among peoples, Peyote meetings, harvesting fruit, gardening, planning for winter—was the time my grandfather spent each morning in prayer or dreams or visions. This was private, even within the family. The effects of this time, nonetheless, were seen in all the ways he helped our family and our clan survive those difficult years.

Kinnikinnick

2 parts wild or domesticated tobacco leaves
1 part sumac or red raspberry leaves
1 part red willow bark (or other willow or dogwood bark)

Leaves: Collect leaves for smoking mixtures in late summer or just before the plant blooms. Hang upside down by the stems in a dry, shaded place. Dry for about a month until semi-dried. When *kinnikinnick* is semi-dried but still just slightly moist, it is optimal for smoking. Store in an airtight container. If the leaves shrivel too much, add an apple piece or dampen slightly. Very dry leaves are harsh to smoke.

Bark: Red willow is the red osier dogwood, *Cornus stolonifera*. It and other dogwoods, as well as willow, provide suitable bark for a smoking mixture. Strip the bark from younger, thin-barked trees or use the inner bark of more mature trees. Dry until only slightly moist. Cut the bark into very thin strips and store in an airtight container. The bark strips are too harsh to smoke alone.

Fruit

In the summer, as gatherers we picked many kinds of berries,
including strawberries, blackberries, raspberries, blueberries,
and cherries. (Wayaka, 2002)

Cherry-picking time was an annual event lasting about two
weeks in July. The people who owned the farms in the area
would send out trucks to transport workers back and forth
from the cherry orchards. When the trucks arrived in our
town, we were ready. Off we'd go, headed for Sturgeon Bay.
(Kaquatosh, 2014)

At every meal, my grandmother would bring out fruit she had
canned. Mostly it was applesauce, because the nearby Catholic
church had apple orchards. After the church left that site in the
1950s because of a fire, the apple trees still bore fruit. Apples are a
lot easier to gather than blackberries and other fruits, so I helped
pick leftover Catholic apples every fall. They filled the basement
storeroom.

Bears and apples would not appear to go together, but they
do. We went apple picking at the orchards where the Wolf River
washed around the bends and eroded small caves. In the autumn
season, bears liked to den in these caves, because they also liked
to harvest the nearby apples. When we went apple picking, it
didn't matter that bears were around, because they did not go after
the same kind of apple we wanted. The bears selected fermented

apples, too rotten for us. The alcohol-laden food must have appealed to them, because they ate to excess. Drunken bears are not hard to identify. They stagger. They roll on the ground with blissful smiles. They slur their growls. Some of the people from the Department of Natural Resources used to say that the bears ate rotten apples only because of the grubs and other protein in them, but that was not true. They ate fermented apples like we would drink apple beer, and they seemed to enjoy themselves until they passed out. We never bothered them.

My aunts also went apple picking, under my grandmother's direction, and then she would supervise the making of jellies, jams, and butters. She thought it was a very good thing for her daughters to learn how to prepare preserves for their future married lives. She was also passing on Menominee traditions of survival through a variety of foods. My grandmother used to make shelves of apple butter. We had it on the table almost every day, but I could eat only so much apple butter.

We always relied on home-canned fruits, even during those times when we were relatively prosperous. Our family routinely made extra cash income as migrant workers. We went to Door County on Lake Michigan to pick cherries or berries for a few weeks each year. We always had some kind of store or business going as a way to keep living above survival level.

In Door County all those years, much interaction occurred among ethnicities. The orchard businesses always put my grandfather on as a foreman, because he could communicate. Those orchard farmers liked the Mexican workers, but they could not speak English, so the farmers could not use them unless they also hired someone like my grandfather. Here he was another kind of leader. I remember my grandfather did not really speak Spanish, but he knew a few Spanish words and Indian sign language. He liked tamales, so he would go to Mexican homes and buy food, to help them financially and also to become friends. He mostly led by example. He would go do something and show others how to do it. So he was a foreman of Mexican groups as well.

One year at Reynolds Orchards, a group of Jamaicans hired on as a crew, and Reynolds, the owner, made my grandfather their foreman. The Jamaicans spoke English better than the white people, my grandfather said, but when whites spoke to them, they gave no sign of awareness. So the white people would tell my grandfather what the Jamaicans should do, my grandfather told them, and they did it. Later, we were back home in Keshena, and that crew of Jamaicans came to visit my grandfather, just a wonderful party of people. I remember voices and foods cooking in the kitchen late into the night. They were on their way home and wanted to come by and visit and see what an Indian reservation was like.

These successful cultural interactions would not have happened without people like my grandfather. If things are not good now, how much worse would they be if people like him had not made these efforts? He was not the only one. There were other elders he looked up to. They learned and taught that building is better than tearing down. If you are shooting at each other, nobody can build anything.

We worked for Reynolds Orchards quite a bit. I remember we would go there and live in the residences they had for the workers—cabins, houses, or barracks. In those days all the picking and grading of fruit was done by hand, so it took a lot of labor. While we worked in Door County, we had a regular supply of fruit for the extended family, which we brought home and preserved. The one kind of fruit that is not valuable commercially is dead-ripe fruit, so the orchard owners gave ripe fruit to the workers. Several barrels of commercially grown apples and cherries also went into our own family larder. Many Indian and white families around the reservation depended on this perk. This stockpiling of ripe fruit was an aspect of Menominee life we were able to continue into the twentieth century.

> "Jimmy Beaver of Neopit has his own way of preserving blueberries. He lays them out on a sheet of birch bark and lets the sun dry them, being careful to take them in at night or when it rains. In about a week to ten days the berries are all shriveled up, and to look at them you would think they were not worth keeping. When it comes to cooking you soak them for a while, just as you would prunes, and use them like any other dried fruit. They are delicious. Jimmy is apt to put a handful in his flapjack batter." (Norick, 1980)

Dried Blueberries

2 quarts fresh blueberries

Wash, sort, and drain blueberries. Be sure stems are removed. Spread on cookie sheets, in one layer. Place in oven overnight on lowest heat. If still moist afterward, continue on lowest heat until the berries are shriveled and barely moist. Store in a cool place or in the refrigerator. Use in cakes, ice cream, cereal, fruit cups, and pancakes.

Cranberry Sauce

1 pint cranberries
2 cups water
½ cup maple syrup (or honey or granulated sugar)

Wash and stem cranberries. Poke each one with a pin, so the berries will not explode when boiled. Bring cranberries and

water to a boil. Stir in syrup or sugar. Keep on a low boil for
10 minutes, stirring to keep from boiling over. Skim off froth.
When the mixture cools, it will gel. Serve with meat.

Cranberries and Wild Rice

1 cup fresh cranberries or ½ cup dried cranberries
½ cup maple syrup (or honey)
¼ cup water
2 cups cooked wild rice

Bring cranberries, syrup or honey, and water to a boil. Simmer
10 minutes to meld the flavors. Pour over the wild rice and
mix well.

Canned Cherries

8 pounds cherries
2 cups sugar (more for sour cherries)

Sterilize jars before canning by placing them in a kettle filled
with water and bringing slowly to a boil. Remove from water
and allow to cool to lukewarm.

Wash, stem, and pit cherries. Drain thoroughly. Pack cherries into four 1-quart canning jars (or eight 1-pint jars). Add ½
cup sugar to each quart jar. Screw lid onto each jar, just tight
enough to be watertight but not screwed tight. Lower into
canning kettle until covered by ½ inch water. Heat slowly to
a boil. Boil for 10 minutes. Remove from kettle with tongs.
Screw lid tight. Check the jars after 24 hours: when the screw
band is removed, the lid should remain sealed tight. Use in pie
fillings or as a meat relish.

Partridge

Partridge Dance Origin—A man who was hunting, long ago, heard what he believed to be a song. He thought that someone was singing and he crept close to the place whence the song seemed to come. When he came close he saw a partridge on top of a log. The partridge was drumming and he had mistaken the sound for a song. He made up a song from the sound which he heard, and also made up the dance to go with it.

Action—Men and women joined in this dance, moving around the drum with arms held widely apart from the sides of the body and moved in the manner of wings.

Song—Partridge Dance Song, recorded by Pigeon: "Pi-na-u tei-tei-ho pi-na-u tei-tei-ho pi-na-u tei-tei-ho pi-nau tei-tei-ho pi-nau."

Translation—Pina'u (partridge) teitei'koho (sounds). (Densmore, 1932)

We had a large family, with grandparents, uncles, aunts, and me, the youngest, a total of nine, but sometimes even twelve of us. It took the hard work of many different people to keep our household maintained and functioning. As many of my uncles were off to the Korean conflict, we needed outside help when muscle work was required. We had a hired hand, Wallace, for many years. His duties were mostly to stack and gather firewood, weed and work in the garden, and mow our considerable-sized lawn. He was a distant relation, perhaps a second cousin who had fallen on lean times. Wallace lived with the family for room and board, in addition to some small cash payments from my grandparents.

Even today, still alive in my memories, I think of Wallace as an interesting person. He was one of the few adults who had time for me. He actually talked to me. Now I realize one of his other jobs was to keep an eye on me.

Mostly, however, I would watch him at his daily work. Wallace taught me to whistle. Because my front tooth was knocked out, whistling was a difficult thing for me to do. But I could soon whistle a couple of different ways. I learned to purse my lips and blow, just like Opie Taylor on *The Andy Griffith Show*. I put my tongue on the roof of my mouth and blew from my throat, making a shrill cry like a blue jay. Or, taking a piece of grass, holding it in between my hands, and blowing across it, I could make a sound like scraping fingernails across a blackboard. Wallace taught me all these techniques. I am sure that our neighbors did not much care for our whistling practice.

Wallace had a tattoo of a hula girl, bare bosomed and wearing a grass skirt, on his arm. It was a real he-man tattoo, and naturally I was intrigued. Wallace was in the Merchant Marines when not living with us on the Menominee reservation. He also served in the US Navy. I remember him saying that he served on a destroyer—this was in World War II. When he flexed his arm muscles he could get that hula girl to dance, really dance, with hips shaking and twisting. Sometimes in my mind I could almost hear tinny Hawaiian music camouflaged among the rustling leaves of the wind—maybe there but not there.

Of course, my grandmother hated this tattoo. Wallace was always careful about wearing a long-sleeved shirt around her. But when he would reach for something, a bowl of wild rice soup, perhaps, I could see the purple flesh of her legs, and the farther he reached, the more her legs were exposed. I did not know then why this image fascinated me. I just knew that someday, I wanted to dance with a bare-bosomed woman in a short grass skirt. I have never had any tattoos, however. I am still afraid of my grandmother.

Once Wallace gave me a bullwhip, hand-braided by him from deerskin. He taught me to make that whip crack. He was an old Indian man even then, and still an important part of my youth, like a bridge, a way to get from here to there, as he taught me the ways of Menominee men.

Wallace was an expert at finding partridge nests along the logging roads, the old foot trails, the granite spaces between the streams and the forests. Partridges are game birds related to pheasants and also ptarmigans, which are indigenous game birds from the high country and the Great White North. All three of these birds nest on the ground. This makes them accessible, but they are well camouflaged, and so almost indiscernible to the human eye. In late spring the partridge nests are filled with eggs, and we would eat them. The eggs are speckled brown and tan, almost invisible when sitting alongside a sandy logging road in the woods. They are about the size of a hickory nut and blend well with their surroundings. Wallace and I, hidden away from Grandma and seated with our backs against some friendly pine tree, ate them raw. After puncturing the top of each eggshell with his thumbnail, he made a straight circular line, peeling off the top fifth of the shell, holding it upright to keep it from spilling. Then we poured the viscous contents into our mouths, swallowing the delicate-tasting egg in one gulp.

Sometimes Wallace took the partridge eggs home for Grandma. Sometimes she would boil them, but mostly she fried them. Grandma fried almost everything. Grandpa always said that one of the few good things that white people brought to us was a frying pan.

Even as a curious child, I did not often find partridges on my own. I could find them only when the female bird would pretend to have a broken wing and draw attention to herself and then lead the predator away from the nest. I learned to recognize that maneuver—birds and other small animals often practice that move. Wallace, however, was able to see those nests from the gravelly roadsides where hens liked to build their nests from twigs and dried fern stalks. Wallace said that these birds do not give off scent when sitting on their nests, and that makes them even safer from the searching gaze of predators, including my family.

Partridge was a staple of our dinner table. Partridges do not migrate, heading south like tourists, so they are available year-round. They resemble most birds—they have wings, drumsticks, and thighs—but their breasts are out of proportion to the rest of their body. A partridge is seemingly all breast and therefore all delicately flavored white meat. I like partridge in wild rice soup. It is the perfect accompaniment to our river-grown, coppery-tasting wild rice.

Partridge meat varies in taste depending on the time of the year due to the birds' diet. In the spring when busy giving birth and raising families, they eat a high-protein diet of insects. Later, in the summer, they eat fruits, seeds, and nuts. In the late autumn and winter, they eat sweet berries off the staghorn sumac and other berries. Their meat in the late summer is sweet because of their diet of blackberries and cranberries. The winter meat naturally has less fat and tastes tangier.

Partridges influenced our music because of their mating rituals. When cold weather ended, people would sit outside and talk. Often drums would come out and songs began. This was the same season, the early summer weeks, when the drumming of partridges thudded across the reservation. After months of severe cold weather, this was a joyous time, as people gathered informally.

Wallace was part of our family group for many years, and he taught me about the outdoors, especially during warm weather. He taught me the best way to eat partridge eggs, whole and raw like oysters. He taught me about a larger world outside the reservation through his hula girl tattoo and war stories. He kept me out of serious trouble, and no doubt he saved my young life from unseen dangers in the woods. Finally one day he quarreled with my grandmother, and he moved in with other relatives, where he no doubt filled the same role. He left me with experience of how to be a Menominee man.

Partridge and Wild Rice

2 cleaned partridges (or 1 duck, 2 game hens, 1 chicken,
    or 1 pheasant)
Soda water
1 tablespoon kosher salt or table salt
1–2 quarts water
1 cup uncooked wild rice
1 cup diced celery
1 large onion, diced
Pepper to taste
4 cloves crushed garlic
1 tablespoon butter

Rinse partridges in soda water, rinse well in clear water, and dry. Put partridges, salt, and water in a soup kettle. Boil 20 minutes. Take partridges out of the water and remove the meat from the bones. Save the bones for stock. Return the meat to the water and add the rice and vegetables. Bring to a boil, lower heat to a simmer, and add pepper, garlic, and butter. Cover and let cook 1 to 1½ hours. Rice should "blossom" when done, with kernels soft and opened.

Roast Duck with Wild Rice Stuffing

~~1 cup cooked wild rice~~
¼ cup diced onion
½ cup mushrooms, diced (optional)
2 tablespoons olive oil or melted butter
1 whole duck (or other poultry)
Soda water
Salt and pepper to taste
1 tablespoon olive oil or butter mixed in 1 cup of hot water
Sugar for browning

For the stuffing, mix together cooked rice, onion, mushrooms, and olive oil or melted butter. (A whole potato or onion may be used in place of stuffing.) Rinse the duck well in soda water, rinse well in clear water, and dry. Rub the inside of the duck with salt and pepper, and fill with stuffing. Tie wings and legs to body with string, then pour hot water and oil mixture over the duck. Cover and bake at 350°F, basting occasionally. When almost done, after about 1 hour, remove cover and return to oven to brown. Sprinkling a little sugar over the skin helps it to brown more quickly.

Survival Hunting

At eve, when the hunters came, they brought in a bear. So then they had a feast. The front and hind feet of the bear, and its head were cooked in one kettle. And the same was done with the fleshy part. When the cooking was done, the head was put into a bowl, and also the bear's hind-paws and fore-paws. (From "Some Adventures of Me'napus," told by Misen Makapiw, in Bloomfield, Menominee Texts, 1928)

Menominee people hunt for subsistence, not sport, and any weapon is acceptable. My grandfather claimed to have used a slingshot until he was thirty, because he was more accurate with it, he said. My grandfather was also given to exaggeration. He was an excellent shot with his .45 caliber semiautomatic military pistol. But shells were expensive, so hunters used them carefully. Slingshots saved money. I do not know if they were used before contact, but my grandfather learned to use a slingshot as a major hunting weapon as a boy at the beginning of the twentieth century. He used inner tubes from car tires to make them.

My family expected me, like all male family members, to hunt as soon as I was able. That meant learning to survive in the forest, which includes many skills. Not getting lost is one, and surviving cold weather is another. From childhood, Uncle Bobby taught me how to stalk, track, kill, and dress animals. My grandfather told me stories that included practical advice. After my frequent misadventures in the woods, he would tell me what I should have done. Avoiding dangerous animals is an important consideration for a hunter, so using a gun to protect myself was part of my training. There were large, fierce dog packs running in the woods in the 1950s and 1960s. When I was small, the family did not depend on my hunting for meals so much as they didn't want me to get mauled or killed by the feral dog pack. The tribe had a bounty of $5 apiece for wild dogs, and that was another advantage to killing them.

Most kids had guns by the age of five or six, and so did I. My grandfather gave me an old .22 pump rifle, but my arms were not long enough to slide the pump. So they found me a bolt action .22. Uncle Billy cut the barrel for me and welded a scope onto it. Originally, the old gun did not have a scope, because real men do not need scopes, but this was like training wheels on a bicycle.

I became a good shot. The men in my family taught me, "Don't point at anything unless you are going to shoot it." I went out squirrel hunting alone for the first time when I was eight years old, and I brought home enough for a meal. I also hunted ducks with that .22 as well as raccoons and porcupines. As my skill increased, I could shoot partridges in flight. A .22 caliber is too small for serious hunting; however, a .22 long rifle is just a little bit smaller diameter than the ammo used in the AR-15's, an assault rifle. It was powerful enough for my purposes.

When I was a little older, my uncles and grandfather taught me that if I saw a deer within shooting distance, I was to kill it. Food was a gift that people had to earn, and the gift may come at unexpected times. When hunting, I learned to aim carefully for a clean kill shot. Deer might seem fleet-footed, but if shot correctly, they will fall over dead on the spot. If I only wounded a deer, then I would have to track it until its death. If a hunter let it go off and die, that was wasteful.

As a hunter, I was taught to be happy that I got food. That is the hunter's prayer. The Menominees in my family did not have a formal prayer, but we were thankful. I have been hunting with white guys, and they are thankful also. I have heard all hunters say they are grateful for the animal giving its life for our food. After a hunter has tracked a deer five miles through a swamp and depleted a ration of ammunition, the deer is an investment. I have tracked wounded game through cedar swamps, and it is not fun. The animal does its best to evade danger. It goes places that people cannot get to easily. When hunters finally do get to the deer, they are thankful, but exhausted. Then it is time to clean the animal and drag it back home. The practice of hunters eating the liver raw comes from how hungry they get. It is soft, fresh meat rich in nutrients.

Once home after killing a deer, time is crucial. Preparing game is labor intensive. We had to remove the organs and bleed the deer. The process included cutting out the scent glands, which are found at the spot behind where the leg bones articulate. Deer run constantly, so they have solid bones. First, I removed unusable parts, like the bottom of the leg bone with the scent glands. The upper leg has thin muscle wrapped around the big bones, and I removed it also. The ratio of deer meat to overall weight is small, but it is still better than small game. A squirrel might have one ounce of meat. After singeing off the fur, it is half the size it was to begin with. Subtract the bones, and that leaves just a thin coating of meat. A deer is normally big enough to feed a family over a couple of days. Dressed-out deer meat would be about ten pounds, still not that much.

When I was young, I thought a deer was a big animal, but it is not, especially on the reservation. A deer is really a big rabbit. It is tasty, and if a deer is available, it is welcome. Venison stew tastes delicious. But comparatively, it is the runty ungulate after bison, then elk. There was this guy on the rez with a huge appetite who could sit down and eat an entire deer. People did not like hunting with him.

For venison stew, my grandmother used bones and other parts of the deer to stretch it out. The venison soup that I had as a kid was made with marrow, not meat. Grandma boiled deer bones to make this thin soup and added macaroni. After the bones boiled an hour or so, she sometimes added tiny flour balls, dumplings, to make it feed all the family. Deer also provided an all-season staple, dried venison.

Bears are another source of meat on the Menominee rez, but I was never much of a bear hunter. I was a good shot, and I did not mind killing a squirrel, a rabbit, or a partridge. Even if it had a soul, it could not be a very big soul. I could not, however, bring myself to kill bear. I did kill one as a young man, and that was enough. It was like killing another man. I have eaten a lot of bear, however, and my relatives still hunt bear. Uncle Bobby got seven bears last year. They are lean and tough, best for stews. They also make good sausage, roasts, meat pies, and fried meat. We are Bear Clan, and once a year we are supposed to get together and eat bear to keep up our connection to the huge animal and the forest that is our home.

My grandfather, born in 1904, remembered bison in Wisconsin when he was a boy. They were wood bison, a different subspecies from the Plains bison. These were not herding animals, nor were they migratory. Bison are an ideal subsistence food source, with up to six hundred pounds of meat from one animal, not counting entrails, bones, skin, and horns. But they are all gone now. I have learned they were close to the same species as those in the grasslands, but the Menominee reservation was the far edge of their territory, perhaps an overlapping region for both subspecies. Animals adapt. Perhaps this bison population adapted to eating cedar. By the time I began hunting, bison were no longer on the reservation.

Fifty years ago, there were fewer deer. There were other species of grazing animals, like elk and bison, but ecological changes in the nineteenth century eliminated these. Then, to fill the void, the deer population increased. White people removed all their predators, including wolves. Deer became the dominant species, putting things out of balance.

Successful subsistence hunting depends on larger animals. If a hunter kills one partridge or one squirrel, it's not enough for a meal. As survival hunters on the Menominee reservation, my uncles and I had to kill dozens of squirrels a day to feed our large family, two per person. Kill a deer, and then hunters have a few days to rest. Only after hunters bring in bison, bear, elk, or deer do people have time to develop art, compose music, and tell stories—to create a culture.

Subsistence living on the rez is possible because of the many sources of meat. Menominee hunters harvest, process, and store deer and bear meat in the fall. Not that it is impossible to get meat in the winter, but in the winter the animal is living off its fat. Deer in the winter will eat everything possible, including cedar. When they start eating cedar, the deer do not taste good. When moose eat cedar the meat still tastes good.

The need for firewood dictated the end of the hunting season. At the end of January, at twenty below zero, people did not have time to go hunting. Instead, searching for firewood took priority. Any time a group of people live together, suddenly there is no firewood within walking distance.

When scholars describe precontact Cahokia, where thirty thousand people lived, they emphasize the amount of fuel needed. Cahokians needed big logs daily for warmth and cooking fires. There had to have been work gangs to support a city of that size. It's hard enough to chop down a tree with a metal axe. Think how hard it would be with a stone ax. This is why Menominees split up into smaller groups in the winter, to maximize resources, especially firewood. In earlier times, winter was trapping season, which took far less energy than hunting. Trappers spend most of the day waiting in a cabin warmed with firewood. Ice fishing is now the deep-winter source for subsistence meat. Small fishing shacks require minimal heating.

I could live in a tent and survive in Wisconsin. Some of my fondest memories are of doing just that. I learned forest survival skills from my uncles, from listening to them talk while they were drinking. They told hunting stories and woods lore as entertainment. I know many wild, edible plants. But is this something I want to do for the rest of my life? I do not think the Indians who want to go back to precontact traditions could do it. They do not know what it is like without a gun and a knife.

On the reservation, seasons dictate the kinds of food available. After New Year's Day squirrels are struggling, and they have no meat on them. The best season to hunt, kill, and eat deer is in the fall, when they fatten up. The same goes for bear, when their store of fat is at its best. The protein is less important than the fat in a cold climate. Apples ripen in the fall also. People eat asparagus and milkweed in the springtime. But hunger knows no season.

Venison Soup

Ribs from 1 deer (about 1–2 pounds; can use other cuts)
1 onion, chopped coarsely
1 bunch carrots, chopped into 1-inch pieces
3 wild potatoes, quartered (or 4 sunchokes, or 1 small
     celery root)
3 stalks celery cut into 1-inch pieces
1 tablespoon butter
½ teaspoon red pepper
Salt and pepper to taste
½ cup uncooked wild rice

In a kettle on the stove, simmer ribs slowly until tender, several hours. Let cool and skim fat. Add vegetables, butter, seasonings, and rice. Bring to a boil, lower heat, cover, and let simmer until rice "blossoms" or opens, about 20 minutes.

Roast Porcupine Dinner

1 porcupine, dressed
5–6 gallons water, divided
¼ cup salt
1 teaspoon baking soda
2 whole peeled onions
½ pound bacon strips
Salt and pepper to taste
12 carrots, peeled and left whole
6 potatoes, left whole

Soak dressed porcupine in a kettle overnight with 2 gallons water and ¼ cup salt. Rinse, then return to the kettle with 2 gallons fresh water and 1 teaspoon baking soda; boil for 20 minutes. Drain. Add fresh water to the kettle, add the onions, and boil 10 minutes. Cut porcupine into portions and arrange in a roasting pan. Remove onions from kettle and add them to the roasting pan along with the bacon. Season with salt and pepper. Add 2 cups water, carrots, and potatoes to the pan. Bake, covered, at 300°F for 2 to 4 hours, until tender. Baste occasionally and add water as needed.

Broasted Rabbit with Wild Onions

2–3 rabbits
2 tablespoons oil
1 clove garlic
Salt and pepper to taste
½ cup cooking oil or bacon grease
½ cup flour
⅔ cup finely chopped wild onions (or chives)

Cut rabbits into pieces and rub with marinade of 2 tablespoons oil, garlic, salt, and pepper. Let marinate 1 hour. Heat skillet to medium high and add ½ cup cooking oil. When it's hot, roll rabbit pieces in flour and brown 5 minutes on each side. Arrange rabbit pieces in a deep baking dish, cover with drippings from the skillet, and sprinkle with wild onions. Bake at 375°F for 1 hour, turning once during cooking time.

How to Cook a Beaver

Where Turtle was camping there were many beavers. So now
Turtle hunted beavers. He simply would take that twine;
from where he was camping he used to dive; he would go
under the water and tie the string to the beavers' legs, there
where they all dwelt. The beavers, you see, are sometimes very
numerous there in their lodges; all of them would Turtle tie
by their legs. Thereupon Turtle used to pull the string up to
the land. Dear me, all the beavers were tied by their legs to
that string! Up on the land Turtle used to bring them. Then
he merely kept hitting the beavers and killing them. (Nehtsi-
wihtuk, in Bloomfield, Menominee Texts, *1928)*

A beaver is not something most people run across in their daily
activities, certainly not in cities, and not even in more rural areas
like the Menominee reservation. The beaver is a water-loving
animal. On the ground it is vulnerable to predators. In the water,
only a large sturgeon, perhaps, would eat a beaver. It comes up
on dry land when it must, but it is never very far from water. It
is a very shy creature. I have never stumbled upon a beaver or
caught a beaver unaware. I have seen beavers, but they are always
going away from me, and I have never sneaked up on one. They
are wary.

Beavers were hunted almost to extinction in many parts of
the United States by both whites and Indians during the fur trade
industry of the eighteenth and nineteenth centuries. Today,

trapping beaver is unlimited on the Menominee reservation for tribal members. Wisconsin and Kansas both allow beaver trapping. In Kansas, where I live, the state reports ten thousand beavers trapped a year, and landowners may trap nuisance beavers at any time. Beaver pelts are still valued, and the meat is palatable.

The beaver pelt was prized over other pelts in the early years of the fur trade. Europeans preferred the beaver, especially for felted top hats. Beaver fur, thickest in the winter, does make a warm garment. Once I was given beaver fur mittens. They were the absolute best pair of mittens I ever had, and even in the subzero weather of the far north, my hands were warm. If I had beaver pelt boots, they would keep my feet warm. They are desirable for clothing in the north, for survival, not as fashion statements.

Beaver trappers are primarily after the pelts, not the food. But most trappers do not disregard the meat of the beaver. Neither whites nor Indians take meat lightly, so generally, the trappers eat the meat. Beavers are large mammals, forty to sixty pounds and more. The body of a beaver is about the size of the body of a white-tail deer. For a successful trapper, the large volume of meat is more than what one family can eat.

Given the variety of game in the woods, certain species are less attractive than others. Some people like the taste of beaver, but to me it is less desirable—though it does taste better than muskrat or raccoon. Rabbit, squirrel, and bear all taste better. Beaver is similar to bear, but beaver meat is much fattier. Beaver swim all day, but they also float around. That helps them add fatty bulk over muscle. Their teeth are good for chewing wood, but they don't eat solid wood. They cut the logs down with their incisors. The logs fall into the water, where the beavers, away from land predators, eat the branches and leaves of the tree. The kind of tree they eat flavors the meat, and some trees, like cedar, add an unpleasant tang.

Beavers use the trees they chew through to build dams and lodges. Dams are made of branches and mud. Beavers use their tails to slap mud on their constructions. They flood areas to put more food in their grasp, and so they interfere with farmers' fields. Beavers also generally make a den in the water, someplace accessible only underwater. In the Menominee creation story, Beaver is the first Woman, and she builds the first home.

If, by chance, a trapper brings you beaver meat, the most desirable part is the tail. Often trappers eat the tails themselves. A beaver tail is a wide muscle. Beavers use it to splash on the water to attract mates, and they use it to slap the ground as competition among males. They use it to signal danger, and they use it to carry mud. Beaver tail resembles beef tongue. It has a layer on the outside that is gristly and tough. That layer can be fatty, but the outer hide is as tough as a scaled hide. This layer of skin is yellow, with octagonal sections, an entire cartilage layer made of those shapes, almost like irregular chain mail. Once the cook gets that off, the inner meat is wonderful.

I watched my Aunt Nita bake pieces of beaver tail in barbeque sauce. The tail can be quite large, so she cut it into manageable sections and put them in a large black cast-iron frying pan. Cast-iron kettles and frying pans are essential to this type of cooking. She added barbeque sauce to the meat, covered it with aluminum foil, and baked it low and slow to make it tender. When it was done, it looked like chunks of dark beef in sauce.

I did roast a beaver on a charcoal grill once. A trapper gave it to me, after removing the tail. We cooked it at my mother's place on a large outdoor grill. It was too big for the oven. It was skinned and gutted—lucky for us, because beaver bones are very bulky. To dress and quarter a beaver is difficult. It is not like dressing out a more manageable lamb or goat. Kitchen utensils are not adequate, so trappers' tools are needed. Curved knives, like scimitars, are used. My daughter's mother and I wrapped up the carcass in

aluminum foil. It took three full days to bake over a fire. We used
four bags of charcoal briquettes. We had a good grill. We could
open it up and access the coal area to add charcoal without removing the beaver. We kept the grill at a low temperature because
that was as much charcoal as the grill would hold.

Cooked beaver has an aroma that I do not find appealing. It
was difficult for me to get past the initial smell. After it cooked
awhile, though, it smelled like good roast meat. Looking at the
final result, it did become roasted meat instead of a beaver carcass.
I ate a plateful, at least a pound, because I had invested so much
time in cooking this creature. My daughter dove into the meat
and loved it. She had no food bias, but I had lived away from
this kind of food for fifteen years, and I had acquired a taste for
beef and processed food. I smothered the beaver with barbeque
sauce; on the rez people often eat both beaver and bear this way.
In retrospect, I should have parboiled the beaver first. My grandmother would have done it that way. I would season it with salt
and pepper, several heads of garlic, and several onions. Then I
would wrap it up in aluminum foil and cook it slowly.

We eat animal flesh because it is easily available. It is easier to
eat a rabbit than to eat a yard full of greens. Maybe it should be
harder to eat meat. When people go into a restaurant and order
prime rib, they are so far removed from that cow. Maybe restaurants should start with choosing a cow, slaughtering it, and butch-
ering it. This would connect people to the individual animal that
dies for them. There are a lot of beaver around my home in Kansas. Were I living close to subsistence, I would not hesitate to eat
beaver from the Wakarusa River. In a subsistence living situation,
people are connected to the land. When I roasted that beaver, I
had almost lost my connection to that era of my childhood and
that culture; my daughter was able to make a new connection in
my place.

Baked Beaver Feast

3 pounds cleaned, skinned, and dried beaver tail or other
   parts
2–3 gallons water
1 teaspoon baking soda
¾ cup flour or cornmeal, divided
2 tablespoons butter (or oil or other cooking fat)
4 apples, cored and quartered
6 carrots, peeled and left whole
6 potatoes, peeled and left whole
3 onions, quartered
2 bay leaves
sugar for browning

Cut meat into serving-size pieces and parboil in a kettle of
water with baking soda. Rinse, drain, and pat dry. Roll the
meat in flour or cornmeal and fry in butter or oil until brown.
Put in Dutch oven or other heavy baking pan with a lid. Add
remaining ingredients. Sprinkle with flour and dot with butter.
Add ½ cup water. Bake, covered, at 350°F until tender. Un-
cover for 20 minutes to brown; sprinkle a teaspoon or more
of sugar over the meat while browning to add extra crispness.

Fishing

*[Manabus] took up his knife and began cutting a small hole
through the tough flesh of Misinimak. When the knife finally
broke through the outer skin and a breath of fresh air came
through the aperture they knew that they were saved and
Manabus quickly enlarged the hole until they all escaped
onto the sand bar on which the great fish was beached. The
Menominees feasted on fresh and salted fish for many moons
and, although the children of Misinimak still frequent our
waters and are occasionally seen by our fishermen they no
longer attack men or animals. (Dillett, 1930)*

*At Sheboygan Falls, Besaw declares, he saw from 10,000 to
15,000 Indians housed in [sic] gathered there to spear the fish
as their ascent of the river was blocked by the falls. (Besaw,
Green Bay Gazette, 16 June 1928)*

The Menominee reservation in northern Wisconsin is a place
people still call Eden. Many times as kids, we did not go home
to eat dinner. Food was in abundance in nature, especially fish.
We would stop to fish at the lake, and if we could not catch them
with reels, we went into the lake and drove the fish to the shore.
Catching fish by hand was easier than fishing. I would jump into
the lake, scooping them and throwing them on land. These were
smaller, but we would catch more, start a fire, and eat them by
the lake.

My people were not trout eaters, originally. We were sturgeon eaters. Sturgeons get big, and the same principle about hunting game of large size applies to fish. It is better to catch one big fish than get a half dozen smaller ones. People say that the little ones are tastier, and maybe that is true, but we were trying to feed our family. One great big fish is more efficient than many small ones.

Because I was a good shot, my grandparents sent me hunting more often than fishing. I was never much of a fisherman, but we ate what I caught. By the age of eight, I was catching fish for family dinners. As soon as my baby daughter Pemy figured out that fish were in the water, and we could catch and eat them, I started fishing more. Almost all the fish we caught we ate within twenty minutes. We had a small grill we often carried with us, or at least tinfoil. We could make a crude grill out of that. Sometimes we put the fish on sticks and roasted them over the fire. We usually carried salt. Nice fat trout are juicy and tasty. Pemy loved them.

There are a lot of places to fish today on the rez, but I suspect the biggest trout are probably fished out. When we were young, my uncles caught fish in the little creek by my grandfather's house. By the time I was in my teens, trout were no longer there, only chubs. But if I was really hungry, I could cook those chubs and smoke them. When they built and dammed Legend Lake, the city of Shawano reversed that stream where it crosses the road, so now it flows north instead of south. That is what keeps Legend Lake at a steady water level. The stream is still flowing many gallons per minute, but the big pools where fish liked to nest upstream are no longer there. My grandfather said right before they built the dam, they measured the depth of the last lake before Legend Lake proper. The sonar could not find the bottom of it. Part of that story he was telling, about not seeing the bottom, was an explanation of where to catch the really big fish. Big fish do not hang out in shallow water.

Behind my mother's house near Neopit, where the bay spreads, there is a hole, and we have caught fish as big as dinner plates, even with the heads cut off. We catch panfish there—sunfish, bluegills, a lot of perch as well. When I was growing up, Lake Michigan still had a lot of perch. That's what was used for diner fish fries. Now restaurants serve only walleye, which are good, but so are perch.

Bass have too many bones. Once I swallowed a bass bone and it got caught in my throat. It hurt badly, and it was hard to breathe. I ate a whole loaf of bread before it dislodged. That's what my family did for me, the cure at the time. We were too far from any emergency room. I have eaten panfish bones also, but they are not so bad. Trout bones cause no problem. Bass have more developed bones, however, and these can cause serious problems.

There are seasons for fishing. Most fish do not bite until after mayfly season. I have fished before May and caught a fish or two, but it is true: they don't really start biting until May. When it is icy cold, fish do not need a lot of food, because they are cold-blooded. As soon as the water warms up, they need more food and start searching for it in shallow waters. Once trout start running and other fish spawn, fishers catch as many as they can, smoke them until they're dried and savory, and store them. On the Menominee reservation, they are a staple.

Boiled Trout

2 whole trout (1½ to 2 pounds), cleaned

1 quart water

1 slice salt pork (bacon or 2 tablespoons butter may be substituted)

1 teaspoon salt

3–4 onion slices

Wash and dry fish. Boil water in a large kettle or stock pot. Add salt pork. Boil for 15 minutes. Add salt, onion, and trout. Cover and simmer gently, about 4 to 5 minutes. Turn off heat and remove pot from heat. Allow trout to steam another 10 minutes. Lift trout out of the water carefully and serve whole.

Baked Walleye

2 whole walleye (1½ to 2 pounds), cleaned
Salt and pepper
½ cup chopped onion
½ cup chopped celery
¼ cup butter or oil
1 cup cooked wild rice or bread cubes
2 tablespoons cream or whole milk
Lemon juice, to taste

Wash and dry fish. Rub insides and outside of fish with salt and pepper. Cook onion and celery in a skillet with butter or oil, until softened slightly. Add rice and cream. Stir until combined. Stuff fish with mixture and place in a large shallow baking pan. Bake at 400°F for 35 minutes until meat is just translucent. Baste frequently with drippings (or extra oil) and lemon juice. Do not overcook. You may substitute a can of cream of celery soup for the onion and celery and mix it with the rice for the stuffing.

Salmon Patties

1 cup fine cubes of soft bread
½ cup milk
1 egg, beaten
1 tablespoon finely diced onion or 1 teaspoon dried onion
    flakes
½ teaspoon salt

½ teaspoon pepper

1 teaspoon dried parsley flakes or 1 tablespoon diced fresh
    parsley (optional)

3 cups canned or thawed salmon or other fish

Oil, fat, or butter for frying

Mix bread, milk, beaten egg, onion, salt, pepper, and parsley.
Fold in flaked fish. Form pancake-size patties with your hands,
about ½ cup each. Heat pan and add ½ inch oil. Fry patties
about 4 minutes until crispy; turn and fry another 3 minutes.

"Frog legs are a delicacy, but frogs are not easy to catch in the
daylight. It has been said that using a long cane pole with a
hook and a strip of red flannel attached to the end is one good
way of snaring them. The Indians wait till night and, with a
light, go down to the shore of the lake. The frogs are attracted
by the light and are easily picked up." (Norick, 1980)

Frog Legs

1 egg, beaten

½ cup flour or cornmeal

2 tablespoons whole milk or cream

1 teaspoon salt

½ teaspoon pepper

Oil for frying

2 pounds cleaned, skinned frog legs

Mix egg, flour, milk, and seasonings together into a batter.
Heat a large shallow skillet, and then add ½ inch oil. Roll frog
legs in batter and drop into heated oil. Fry 15 minutes, until
crispy; turn and fry until golden brown, about 5 minutes. Do
not overcook.

Manomin, *Good Seeds*

*According to Menomini tradition, the wild rice, since it springs
up from under the earth and the water, is the gift of one of the
Underneath beings, probably* Sekdtcoke'maii. *The Indians
believe that the birds on their migrations follow these beings
and bring rice to them. They sometimes, though seldom, intro-
duce the plant to new waters. (Skinner, 1921)*

*As soon as the first lot of rice has been thus prepared for
eating by each family, the harvesters gather about and their
leader offers tobacco, saying: "I thank thee, Rice-maker
(Ono'miahawdtuk), that we have lived, to see this season.
As we must not partake of thy bounty without tobacco and a
ceremony, I am doing this faithfully to carry out our part, to
thank thee, and to fulfil thy wishes before we touch and taste
the rice, in order that we may be successful in making a good
harvest." When the leader has made this speech, the feast
begins. (Skinner, 1921)*

ma'noman, *wild rice.*
nemdkosku'tcikutdo, *wild rice threshed by the feet.*
apu'atdo, *parched wild rice.*
anapa'kwun, *an underground cache (also called wana'kun)
for wild rice. A hole dug in the earth about the size and
shape of a barrel, and lined with basswood- or elm-bark.
The rice is placed in bark-fiber bags wrapped in rolls of*

> *the same material. Corn was cached in the same way, and*
> *kettles of maple syrup were covered and hidden likewise.*

meii ko'ne ata so, *a canoe filled with wild rice or corn and*
buried in a hillside for better drainage. (Skinner, 1921)

Meno is the Menominee word for good, and *min* is grain, seed, or berry, so the word means "good grain" or "good seed." The Menominee Tribe of Wisconsin is named for this—*ee* means people, so we are the Wild Rice People. Wild rice is the tribe's primary vegetable, used to supplement a diet of fish and game. This foodstuff is ubiquitous throughout the Algonquin-speaking region. An Ojibwe band in Wisconsin is named for wild rice, Manoominikeshiinyag, the "Ricing Rails" band, now known as the St. Croix Ojibwe. In Minnesota, across the river, that same band is part of the Milles Lacs, or Thousand Lakes, Ojibwe, and those lakes contain rice beds. So there is a Menominee band of Ojibwe in Minnesota, but distantly related.

The Menominee language is Algonquian, related to Ojibwamowin, but the two tribes separated some time ago. The Menominee language comes from around the Hudson Bay area and southward, so it is most closely related to Cree. My Grandfather Moon visited the Hudson Bay area, and he said Menominee and Cree speech are almost identical. The difference is akin to northern and southern American accents. Thus, *manomin* unites people as well as language.

Many people use wild rice—from the Atlantic and across the Ohio and Mississippi River Valleys, the Hudson Bay area, and west of the Great Lakes—so its importance cannot be underestimated. It unites many peoples with a shared food culture. It is like wheat flour to North America, corn to the Southwest and to Mexico, and rice to southern Asia. It gave Algonquin-speaking peoples of the northern lakes and rivers a common food and time frame to develop cultures.

Manomin was a major trade item during the fur-trading years. The French called it *folle avoine,* "fool" or "wild" oats, and they recognized it as a food source and adopted it at first historic contact. French voyageurs depended on local Indians to supply them with food as they traveled, through trade. This stable winter food source made the cash trade in furs possible. When stored away from vermin, it keeps indefinitely, and it is nutritious, filling, and easy to carry.

Menominees live at the intersection of three Indigenous regions with different staples. The western prairies had big game, including antelope, deer, elk, and bison. My grandfather, born in 1904, remembered a few wood bison on the Menominee reservation, and before his time they ranged north of Lake Winnebago. A second major region of the crossroads was eastern, where farming produced beans, squash, sunflowers, and Indian corn. The waterways of the Great Lakes, the third region, had fish and wild rice. Wild rice grows in the shallows of lakes and in slow-moving river bends, and even in brackish waters near the sea, so it was widespread. It grows from Manitoba to Florida, but it flourishes in the northern swamps. The Menominee people used all these foods, and all combine well with wild rice—meat, fish, and berries.

The different wild rice locations have distinguishing characteristics, and in time, people's use of it affected its varieties. This is basic Darwinian law: diversity in habitat affects diversity in form. People selected wild rice strains for certain characteristics, such as a short growing season. Each area, from the headwaters of the Mississippi to the Great Lakes to the Ohio, has a difference in salinity, sunlight (river valleys lined by trees have more shade than open prairie lakes), water temperature, and soil. Wild rice grows in many watery environments.

I have picked wild rice on the Wolf River, and it is slightly reddish because of the copper content of Wisconsin soil. It is shorter and the grains are fatter. Its harvest season is earlier than that of lake rice, so it requires a shorter growing season. In the northern range of the plant, the rice is even smaller and cooks more quickly, important for areas where fuel is scarce.

People manipulate the plants as they harvest the rice, so after generations it evolves. When ripe, a knock is all that is required to shake ripe seeds off the stalks. The harvester has two sticks or knockers, one to bend the stems over the flat boat edge and the other to whack the stems to release ripe seeds. A tarp spread in the bottom of the boat catches the seeds and casings. When spikelets are dried and agitated, the chaff is light and easily removed by the wind. Finally, the clean wild rice can be parched slightly. It dries for storage relatively quickly. Thousands of years have created a wild rice optimal for harvest in different habitats. Wolf River rice requires a stronger knock to be harvested, as the current constantly keeps pressure on the plant, making it hardier. Years of harvest have created a selection for certain characteristics, and ripe river rice clings to the stem more than lake rice.

Ojibwe people harvest rice along the shores of lakes, where more sunlight is available. Lake wild rice is long and thin, light in color, and the plants are taller. French sources from the seventeenth century describe seven-foot-tall wild rice plants that clogged the shallows. This rice is sweeter, with an iron taste. Ojibwe use canoes and other lake boats, so they favor the taller, more flexible rice stalks that can be bent over the bow of the canoe and seeds knocked in easily. In time, this preference favors the growth of taller plants, as the harvesting process spreads stray seeds about a lakebed.

The city of Shawano, including a chain of lakes, was once Menominee territory. Local timber barons constructed a dam for a paper mill. It and the related railroad construction disrupted river traffic, animal passage, and vegetation. Before this section of the Wolf River was dammed, the shallows were prime ricing areas. Raising the water levels flooded the rice patches. Wild rice is very responsive to the environment, including the purity and level of the water. The loss of this area to the white developers in the 1870s not only a was blow to the Menominee people but also diminished wild rice diversity.

As a young boy, I saw an old Menominee man, always alone, drag a flat-bottomed skiff along the Wolf River to harvest wild rice. This craft would be the equivalent of the traditional dugout canoe, or *bateau,* not a birch bark canoe. The canoes on display in the Menominee and Stockbridge-Munsee museums are wooden dugouts. These boats were used as utility trucks, while the swifter and more maneuverable bark canoes were like motorcycles. This type of wooden skiff, with cedar bark mats or tarps laid in the bottom, was ideal for collecting rice.

The man, as I watched, waded in hip boots along the shore and towed the boat, knocking the rice in with two sticks. He stayed in the slower-moving parts of the river, but still, the rice he harvested in moving water was different from lake-grown rice. The man often caught minnows in the same fashion, to sell for bait, so he was familiar with the river and avoided deep holes or rapids. As he waded, he also looked for nodules of copper, which he sold. In the 1950s and early 1960s, copper could still be found in the Wolf River. His harvesting method was optimal for river wild rice.

When my daughter Pemy was a small child, I remembered how that man had waded the Wolf River to harvest wild rice. So I put her in a backpack carrier and waded the slow parts of the river, putting ripe wild rice grains in my pockets. Each plant produces quite a bit, so it did not take long to fill my pockets. The next time, I took cloth bags and filled them. At home, I put the rice in an airy place, on top of the refrigerator, where it dried out. After a few days, I took it outdoors, rubbed it between my hands, and the slight breeze blew away the chaff. That was all it took to prepare it to eat.

We ate a lot of wild rice when I was growing up, stewed with pork, often ham hocks. The obvious pairing with wild rice is waterfowl. I preferred it cooked with wild partridges, as the meat was sweeter. When cooked with partridge, it makes a very low-fat dish. Wild rice is a low-fat, high-fiber food, a healthy grain, with six grams of protein in each cooked cup. Wild rice also contains B vitamins, iron, and other minerals.

My mother cooked wild rice often, as a regular part of our meals, instead of potatoes. She called it survival food and told us how it helped Menominees get through famines of the long northern winters. Wild rice expands to four times its size, so rice soup feeds more people with less meat. The ingredients can include one or two partridges instead of six. Pork from the grocery store makes a rich stew, and wild game with high fat content are bear, beaver, and porcupine. These create a richer stew.

The basic recipe is to put three parts water to one part rice in the kettle, boil, and add salt, pepper, and cut-up pieces of uncooked meat. Then cover it and let it simmer for an hour or so, until the rice opens and the meat is cooked through. It can be kept warm on the stove all day. Wild rice goes with both sweet and savory accompaniments. At Native American Church tipi meetings, wild rice was the expected food for breakfast. It was boiled with fresh water in a kettle until the grains popped open, then served with butter, blueberries, maple sugar, and salt. These were the four Menominee food groups—water, meat, sweet, and salt. Wild rice was like meat or beans because of its protein content.

We had both "good seed" grains, wild rice and corn, but wild rice was the more traditional Menominee food. Because it was not farmed, the Menominees were free to move to follow the hunting, fishing, and berry-picking seasons. The same was true for ricing season. Indigenous people cultivated wild rice by leaving some for the animals and by spilling some of the harvest. Seeds in the bottom of the boat would fall out in nearby places on the river, and the next year, another patch would grow. So the crop spread year by year. It's likely this became intentional, as with so many varieties of cultivated corn that exist across the Americas.

Native cultivation of wild rice differs from white agriculture. First, it is not a monoculture crop. Monoculture is the practice of reducing a variety of crops to one, like potatoes or wheat. Wild rice is among the range of grains used by Menominees. Second, the crops were selected to grow in a natural setting. No need to plow up acres of land and disrupt the natural order. Third, Indian cultivation is designed to produce the greatest amount of food with a minimum of labor. For example, Pawnee people would plant corn, beans, squash, and sunflowers on the flood plain and sandbars of the Republican River after spring floods. Then they would leave their crops to follow bison and other game. When they returned in the fall to collect their crops, everything was ripe. They did no weeding.

Another example of this is the Mexican jungle. John Hoopes, a professor at the University of Kansas and a specialist in Middle American cultures, described how the word *jungle* brings to mind random vegetation. In fact, jungles are great food-producing areas with optimal spacing. The biomass is greater than in monocultures—greater than the sum of the individual plants. Hoopes understood that jungles were planted. Great Mayan cities were in jungles, a natural setting. Plantings provided a diverse diet. Estimates of the American population before contact are up to sixty million people, scattered across the continents. Conquistadors did not hack into forgotten, lost cities. They followed trade trails that wended among productive forests and grasslands. Turkey feathers and shells were traded all over—nobody lives in isolation. If we did, people would have to learn everything new, like which mushrooms are poisonous. Knowledge spread along with traded foods and goods. When I moved to Kansas, people did not need me to tell them about wild rice.

Agriculture is for personal gain, cultivation is for subsistence. Monoculture is a logical outgrowth of agriculture—how better to create a biological factory for profit? This is one of the most important differences between Native and European traditions. Wild rice grows and is used; it is not a profitable crop. Like amaranth, a neglected grain, it is found all over. You do not need a cash-based system to acquire it.

For the Menominees, wild rice ripened in the late summer to early fall, so it could be harvested at a time between sturgeon fishing and late fall deer hunting. Cultivation of bison in the grasslands regions followed a similar pattern. *Bison antiquus* was not a migrating animal. The current descendants, the prairie "buffalo," would migrate after years of prairie burnings by Indigenous peoples who learned to set fires to create more pasture. New grass in the spring is tender and nutritious, so the bison learned to move into areas with new growth. This altered the bison's behavior, but it did not domesticate it.

Wild rice appeared at the edges of glaciers as the great ice retreated, and the glaciated pools and moraines, along with cool, damp weather patterns, created perfect conditions for its growth. According to archaeological records, Copper Culture hunters, ancestors of the Menominees, butchered mastodon near the reservation more than eleven thousand years ago. The habitat for mastodons is perfect for wild rice. Today it continues to grow undisturbed in the tundra and far northern waterways.

People need plants to complete their diets, so wild rice made it possible for a larger population to live in the northlands. Because it can be dried and stored, it can be stockpiled. Menominees, as well as all Woodlands nations, take respites from hunting for a daily food supply. This gives them time to tell stories and create magic. They do not simply survive; they prosper. Before a culture can take root, the storytellers need to be fed. Without surplus food, there is no culture. Wild rice made the Menominee life possible.

Wild Rice Stuffing

1 cup uncooked wild rice
3 cups salted water
½ onion, diced
½ cup diced celery
1 tablespoon butter or oil
2 cups stale bread cubes
¼ cup melted butter
2 teaspoons salt
2 teaspoons dried sage or ¼ cup chopped fresh sage

Cook wild rice in water by bringing to a boil in a kettle on the stove, covering, and simmering 20 minutes or until the grains "blossom." Drain. Sauté onion and celery in 1 tablespoon butter or oil. Mix cooked wild rice and remaining ingredients together, stirring melted butter in well. Use to stuff poultry, game, or other meats.

Wild Rice with Squash

½ cup dried, sweetened cranberries
4 tablespoons butter or oil, divided
3 cups cooked wild rice, salted
3 cups cooked and peeled winter squash (cut into 3-inch chunks)
Salt and pepper to taste

Soak cranberries 15 minutes in ¾ cup water and drain, reserving water. Heat a large skillet to medium high and add 3 tablespoons of the butter. Melt. Add cranberries, rice, and squash. Stir and simmer until heated through and liquid is absorbed, about 4 minutes. Stir in 1 tablespoon butter, salt, and pepper. Serve warm.

Wild Rice Casserole

2 cups uncooked wild rice

6 cups water

1 teaspoon salt

2 tablespoons butter or olive oil

½ cup diced onion

½ cup diced celery

1 cup sliced fresh mushrooms (or canned mushrooms)

1 can cream of mushroom soup (or 1½ cups roux)

Cook wild rice with salt in water by boiling in a large kettle, covering, and reducing to medium heat to simmer for 15 to 20 minutes, until not quite done. Drain. Sauté vegetables in butter while the rice cooks. Add vegetables and can of soup to nearly cooked wild rice. Stir well. Bake in a casserole dish at 325°F for 30 minutes.

Corn

At last the leader saw something standing on the plains. He and his men hurried to the spot and found something unlike anything they had ever seen before. "This is corn," said the leader. "We will call it Wapi'min *(white kernel)." The others agreed that they had heard of it and that it was good to eat, and they all tasted it. It was good, and they brought home some seed. When they got home, they waited until spring and planted the corn so it could grow. This is how the Menominee got corn. (Brown, 1940)*

ina'n wa' pimin, *white corn.*
ape'sa'pimin, *black or "blue" corn.*
kinu'putemin *(long white kernels), white man's corn.*
osauwa'pimin, *yellow dent.*
nani'sapimin, *popcorn.*
sewa'pimin, *sweet corn. (Skinner, 1921)*

My grandmother cooked not wild rice but another seed crop, corn, because she was Catholic. She grew up with the more assimilated group on the reservation. Also, because of her work schedule she did not have time to participate in the time-consuming ricing process. Farming people sold corn to the family, or Grandpa grew it in the garden.

We ate colored Indian corn, or flint corn, until I was a teenager. At that time, in the 1960s, white farmers brought sweet corn into the area. Highway 29, which runs along the southern border of the Menominee reservation, is the dividing line between the prairie and the northern forest, with colder weather to the north making corn cultivation problematic. The growing season is too short for most corn, although certain varieties did grow north into Canada. This new sweet corn just barely ripened in time for harvest. I remember best the colorful Indian corn grown when I was a child, which was more dependable. My grandfather managed to coax a crop from the garden every year.

Different varieties of corn go into different meals. Flint corn is best for hull corn, or lye hominy, made by boiling hardened kernels in lye. In the old days, ashes were boiled with two parts water to create lye, then settled, and then the dried corn was boiled in the strained water. This removed the hulls, so a softer inner kernel remained for soup. Hull corn soup is the same recipe as wild rice soup. In many recipes, dried corn can be substituted for wild rice. Another way my mother and aunts prepared corn was to dry it into raisin-size kernels. This concentrated the sugar. The kernels can be added to a stew as a sweetening agent. The drying process is easy to do on cookie sheets in a low-heat oven. We ate cornbread often as well.

Something Indians don't like to talk about is how the Peruvian people grew corn five thousand years for beer before they started eating it. It's true; Native people had alcohol long before contact with Europeans. Corn must be cultivated to become a productive, domesticated food source, as it does not occur without human intervention. At some point in precontact history, then, corn became a food and traveled throughout the Americas.

In the 1920s, anthropologist Alanson Skinner recorded many corn recipes on the Menominee reservation. Apparently, my grandmother's was not the first generation to prefer the cultivated crop. Corn was a shared food with neighboring white farmers, so it put people into relationship with each other on many levels.

Menominees have no prohibited foods, so both wild rice and corn are good choices for food staples. I grew up with both.

"Popcorn, called *nani'sapimtn*, 'mouse corn,' or 'little brother,' was also raised. It was usually prepared by roasting or parching, and pounding it in a mortar, with the addition of dried meat, maple sugar, or wild rice, or all three. In this condition it was very nourishing. . . .

"Another popular dish is prepared by scraping the green corn from the cob with a tool made from one of the unworked rami of the inferior maxillary of the deer. The kernels, which are considerably broken up by the scraping, are put in a birch-bark pan or dish. Grease is added and thoroughly mixed with the corn, which is molded into cakes and baked in the ashes." (Skinner, 1921)

Cornbread

1½ cups cornmeal
½ cup wheat flour
2 teaspoons salt
2 teaspoons baking soda
1 egg, beaten
1 tablespoon melted butter (or oil)
¾ cup water, milk, or sour milk for a tangier bread

Mix dry ingredients together. (Add another teaspoon baking soda if sour milk is used.) Add egg, butter, and enough water or milk to make a thick batter, about ¾ cup. Put in a greased 8 × 8-inch baking pan and bake at 350°F until the center springs back when touched, about 35 minutes. For variation, add ½ cup whole corn kernels or diced green pepper.

Venison and Dried Corn Soup

4 quarts water
Neck, ribs, and shoulder of a deer
2 cups dried corn
1 tablespoon salt
1 tablespoon butter
2 teaspoons pepper

Heat a 5-quart kettle on the stove and add the water. Add remaining ingredients, bring to a boil, lower heat, and cook on medium heat until meat is tender and falling off the bone, about 3 hours.

Corn Soup

1 quart sweet, dried corn
4 pork hocks (or any fatty meat cut)
1 teaspoon pepper

Soak corn in 4 quarts cold water for 2 hours. Drain. Add corn to 4 quarts boiling water. Lower heat and cook 1 hour. Add pork hocks and pepper. Cook 2 hours on medium heat until meat is tender.

Maple Syrup

*An event of the sugar camp and of all large gatherings is the
beggars' dance (ana'mowin). At evening, toward the end of
a sugar camp, a party of men and women start out with one
man carrying the drum. They stand in front of a wigwam
and sing and dance. The people understand their purpose
and invite them to enter. The leader of the party is given
maple sugar and three or four members of the party have
bags in which to carry it away. . . . After receiving these gifts
they dance again, and if they cannot complete the round of
the camp in one evening they finish the next night. This dance
is in four parts, each with its songs. (Densmore, 1932)*

*Maple sugar, traditionally stored in birch-bark cones, is used
to season meat, vegetables, manoomin, and berries all year
long. Smoky, grainy, subtle, or strong—varied like wines—
real Ojibwe maple syrup (zhiiwaagamizigan) or sugar cakes
(ziiga-iganan) borrow their taste from the bark containers
and the wood fires used to cook down the sap. (Erdrich, 2013)*

Sugar camp is a cultural practice in the northern woods of
Wisconsin. The camp itself and all the activities are called the
"sugar bush." Indians and white people and blacks all call this
"sugar bush." It would be very interesting to see if the Hmong,
as the newest group of immigrants in northern Wisconsin, pick
up the practice of "making sugar bush."

Langlade County and Menominee County—including the towns of Wausau, Shawano, Keshena, Neopit, and Zoar—are sugar bush country. Our forest is a mix of hardwood and softwood. When my grandparents were young, the forest was predominately elm, but elms died off during the Dutch elm disease epidemic. Sugar maples were always present. They grow freely among the conifers.

Across ethnic groups maple sugar is important for its food value, but more importantly because it represents springtime. Sugar bush is the first time people get together after scattering for the winter. The season begins when sap runs during the daytime but the temperature still drops to freezing at night. The sequence of seasons begins earlier in the south and spreads north, so the time of making maple sugar begins earlier in Neopit than it would in Quebec. It is the first sign of the forest coming back to life after subzero temperatures.

Sugar maples are incredibly beautiful. They are prolific. My grandparents used to sell wood for bowling pins to a company in Chicago. The best wood, they said, is sugar maple. They would cut an eighteen-inch chunk out of a trunk. Each blank had to be six by six. They would sell those blanks to the company to finish into pins by putting the blanks on a lathe. My grandparents were not the only ones to sell maple wood. This was a big business on the rez.

White people make maple sugar on their own property. When Menominee people make sugar bush, it is made on shared, public property. If a family had a maple sugar camp in a particular part of the rez in the past, people would consider it to be that family's sugar camp. Even though there was no title to the land, it being tribal land, people still recognized each family's historic use of the land.

My grandfather's sugar bush camp was Dutchman's Hill, between Zoar and Neopit, the hill that overlooks the Mill Pond and

Race Horse Rapids. All along this area, from where those rapids start to where the river becomes placid, is sugar maple growth. As a kid, I knew that place as Dutchman's Hill, and it never occurred to me to question how some place on the rez become known for a Dutchman. The story is this: Charlie Dutchman was not one hundred percent Native, and the "Dutch" refers to his "Deutch" or German ancestry. Charlie is buried in the Neopit cemetery, not in the Catholic part, but in the trees, way beyond the boundary. Many people knew him, white and Indian, since he lived right on the trail that begins in Chicago and makes its way around Lake Superior. Many people considered him a great sorcerer, a man who used magic to get his will done. This hill was named after him. He did not live on the hill, but on the field across the road. The field was named after him too. This was one of the northern-most reaches where corn could grow. My own grandparents had a small farm not far from Dutchman's Field.

I once asked my Uncle Buddy if there was anything that ever scared him. He replied that Dutchman's Field was the one place he feared. He said as a kid, when he walked from Zoar to Neopit and back, he went right through that trail. He would run because it scared him. Its geographic location is near the Wolf River and other small, fast, cold bodies of water. Because of the moisture, it often gets foggy. That probably contributes to the ambiance.

My grandfather would tap maple trees on Dutchman's Hill, just above the feared field. When people tap a tree, pounding a spigot into it, they are wounding the tree. Sap is the blood of the tree, its life substance. That leaks out, and the goal is to collect that life essence, to use it and not waste it. Trees contain a vast amount of fluids within them, not just a quart of sap, or people would not bother. There are dozens, perhaps hundreds, of gallons of moisture within a tree, depending on the location. If a tree is next to a river, perhaps a ton of sap flows in just one tree. Sap weighs eight pounds a gallon, sometimes more. Other substances are within the sap, so it weighs more than water. That large volume of sap needs to be boiled to distill the water out. Sugar makers boil it in open containers so the nonsugar part of the sap, the water, evaporates.

The object is to collect the sap, boil off the water, and collect the concentrated syrup. The ratio of water to sap indicates quality. Laws specify what commercial sellers can call grade A, grade B, and so forth. The grades range from colorless to dark brown. The darker the syrup is, the more valuable, since there is less water. It is incredibly sweet.

The process of making the syrup takes a lot of energy. The extended family tends the fire, with large amounts of wood to keep the container boiling. This boils all day, from dawn until nightfall, when everyone goes to bed. Given the laws of thermodynamics, it becomes so very hot that it remains warm even overnight.

The most efficient way to make maple syrup is not small batches, but a hundred or more gallons at once. This can be done indoors with the proper facilities. When we had a house on the lake in Keshena, we tapped maybe twenty gallons, which we put on the stove in a big canning pot. As it evaporated, we added more sap. We boiled it three or four days. All the wallpaper within ten feet of the stove came off the wall, steamed by the humidity.

Once the maple syrup is made, it has to be processed for storage. It will not last in a dirty bottle with a cork in it. It has to be sterilized. When people "put up" maple syrup, they are really canning it, putting a sterilized product in a sterilized container and sealing it with a sterilized lid. If the syrup is contaminated, in a week it turns into maple brandy. It makes a very heady brandy very quickly. Obviously the old Indians knew this. Nonetheless, this was not an important type of intoxicant, but rather an important food group, one of the four Menominee food groups of water, meat, sugar, and salt.

How to keep syrup from spoiling? One method is to put it

somewhere and allow a layer of mold to grow on top of it. That seals the syrup below it. I asked my grandparents how they stored it before pasteurization, and that was the answer. Sealing by canning is another method.

My grandfather also made a lot of maple candy. It is an extravagance. This process removes 99 percent of the water, and it becomes a hard thing that resists breakage. A little bit goes a long way because it is so concentrated. It was probably a barter good, with a standard price. I base this on observation. Wherever maple sugar was made in the old days, the metal molds were a standard size. Perhaps the Hudson's Bay Company standardized them, perhaps it was earlier.

Making maple sugar candy was dangerous. First, getting the sap to boil was a dangerous process, because it involves fire. Boiling sugar is volatile, like boiling oil. It is viscous and sticks to skin. Sugar is flammable, and people could catch fire if they were not mindful. Even the pouring process was dangerous. Candy makers must pour boiling fluid into small molds, presumably greased with something—adding more danger. These are my memories, from when I was five or six, so I can't remember if they greased these or not. But they must have.

My grandfather loved maple syrup. I cannot remember a time when we did not have some form of maple sugar, either dried or in syrup form, in the house. One reason is he loved a winter squash he grew, Hubbard squash. Like potatoes, squash is a food that can be stored. Hubbard squash in the local grocery store are puny compared to what my grandfather grew. He grew basketball-size squash. He was feeding a large family, so it was easier to prepare large squash rather than dozens of little ones.

He would cut the squash into three-inch-square pieces and put them meat side down in a baking pan, pour enough maple sugar to cover all the meat, and bake it. He liked that better than pumpkin pie, even. It was not a dessert, even though it was sweet.

We ate it once or twice a week, served with mashed potatoes, meat, and vegetables.

One sugar camp, I took a friend with me early in the morning before my grandparents arrived. My grandmother would not make coffee out of maple sap, so we had to be early. Because it was a huge fire, with a large volume of sap, the fire had not gone out during the night. We made coffee straight from the hot sap, and it was good. We could taste a different flavor. It was not highly sweet or maple-like, but we could taste a savory difference. It was like blood of the tree. Maybe blood is a cold word, but it is a life essence.

Some Menominee families, like those near Bear Trap Falls, worked larger groves of maple trees to have some left over to sell. They were more traditional Big Drum people. Their large camp was more of a celebration, with far-flung family members getting together for the first time after winter. Hunters and trappers would be home to help out, after spending the cold season at small hunting camps in the distant bush. No matter what tradition, some of my earliest memories are of the sugar bush and the friendly gatherings in late winter as we camped out in the woods.

It was white people who looked at forests as dark and faintly evil places filled with witches who eat little boys and girls. I have never met an Indian who thought that way. I and every other kid heard all the time from our parents, "Go out and play in the woods." No one thought twice about danger—we could drown, fall off a cliff, have a tree fall on us, meet a rabid wolf, eat a poisonous berry. Menominee kids still go play in the woods, just as their parents did. The woods are more home-like than wooden houses. As Menominees, we make a living in the woods. We get food from the woods. Exercise is moving through the woods. Entertainment is the woods. So who is a Menominee person? The woods. We represent that spiritual essence, one and the same. We are, like the sugar maples, aspects of the woods.

Maple Custard Pudding

(Sylvester Norick)

4 cups evaporated milk, heated to scalding
⅔ cup maple syrup
¼ cup cornmeal
2 tablespoons flour
1 teaspoon salt
½ tablespoon bacon grease, venison fat, or butter
¼ teaspoon ginger or nutmeg
¼ teaspoon cinnamon
1 cup whole milk

Cook all ingredients except whole milk in a saucepan over medium heat until they thicken, stirring constantly. Pour into a baking dish. Add milk without stirring. Bake at 325°F for 2 to 3 hours. Serve with cream and chunks of maple sugar.

Maple Candy

2½ cups maple syrup
¾ cup walnuts or other nuts

Boil maple syrup to soft ball stage (235°F). Remove from heat and stir until syrup changes color. Add nuts and combine thoroughly. Quickly pour into a buttered 9 × 13-inch pan. Cut into small pieces. Allow to cool completely before removing from pan. Dried cranberries or blueberries can be used as variation.

Popcorn Balls

1½ quarts popped popcorn, popped with hot air or oil
½ cup dried squash seeds (optional)
1½ cups maple syrup

Place popcorn and squash seeds in a sturdy pot or bowl. Boil
maple syrup in a 2-quart saucepan to 260°F. Pour the boiling
syrup over the popped corn and squash seeds. Let cool until
warm. Butter your hands and shape popcorn mixture into
balls the size of tennis balls.

Greens

A Few Herbs and Their Uses—Maidenhair fern (Adiantum pedatum; *literally: "That which looks like a stag's horn"*). *It is a medicine. One eats of it when one is going hunting. Bloodroot* (Sanguinaria canadensis; *literally: "Keeps flowing forth"*). *It is a dye; when rushes are dyed with it, the effect is pretty. The root is used. Spikenard* (Aralia racemosa; *literally: "Morning Star Herb"*). *It is a herb-medicine good for burns.* (Maskwawanahkwatok, *in Bloomfield*, Menomini Texts, *1928*)

First greens in the spring are ferns and dandelions, then asparagus, then milkweed. Skunk cabbage may be the very first green to appear, but my family did not eat it. On the rez are many edible ferns. Fiddleheads, curled-up shoots of ferns, are not that delicious. They are slimy, mucilaginous, and furry. The ostrich fiddlehead fern is edible—not poisonous. I could not eat a pot full. When I was a young man living off the forest, I ate them raw, also, but well washed. I remember eating fiddleheads with fresh-caught trout. We just ate them plain. They can also be thrown into salads for texture. Sometimes we had them steamed with butter. They turned bright green—all wild greens turn bright green when cooked. They do not taste bad, but they are different. It is like eating okra. Euell Gibbons, who wrote *Stalking the Wild Asparagus*, said they could be used as a thickener in stews like gumbo. My grandfather knew of them, but he did not seek them out. Some people still eat them, but fewer do today.

Despite their abundance, Grandma did not cook with greens. My grandparents ate meat. That was the center of the meal, and all the accompaniments were canned, usually from our garden or from our regular foraging spots. People ate cabbages when I was growing up, and these lasted most of the winter. Sauerkraut lasted all winter, and I always thought it was Menominee food. Grandpa had cabbage in his garden because it is hardy. The first fresh food in the woods, though, is greens.

Dandelions emerge before fiddleheads. Dandelions can be steamed like spinach and also eaten raw in salads. We picked young shoots before they turned bitter. Wild onions are on the rez. I've smelled them but not picked them. My grandfather knew where asparagus grew and knew all about it, even though it was not his choice to gather and eat. Lots of people would gather asparagus, both Indian and whites. Wild asparagus is much different in size than store-bought. Wild asparagus has very thin stalks. To me, it tastes much better. It tastes buttery, whereas cultivated asparagus does not. I cannot remember putting butter on wild asparagus, even in Wisconsin, a dairy state. It grew all over, often on sides of roads. All wild asparagus used to be cultivated, and it escaped into the wild. I have found asparagus growing on the tops of windswept hills, in heavy pine forests, and in swamps. I have found it along rivers and in cracks in granite boulders. It also grows around towns like Keshena, but I have found it in every microclime of the reservation. When I was a young man, I asked my grandfather about asparagus and its growing habits, and he was very knowledgeable about it.

I decided to use greens after I read Gibbons as a young man, so I started looking for wild foods on the rez. I was from that generation. I would rather get organic natural food than homogenized, commercialized, packaged food. People still talk about my daughter's mother on the Menominee reservation because she knew more about the use of natural plants than anyone else. That knowledge was almost lost. The rapidly rising diabetes rate is directly attributable to diet. We did not know for sure in the 1970s and 1980s, but we suspected health and food went together.

That part of Wisconsin has such a variety of food. Milkweed is edible, and tasty, but you have to boil it three to seven times to get the sticky, white, waxy sap out of it. Never eat anything with white sap, because it is usually poisonous. Milkweed is the exception, but it must be prepared correctly. Starting with ice-cold water, bring milkweed pods to a boil, then throw away the water. Taste the pods to see if they are bitter. Some milkweed is sweet after doing that twice. I've had some milkweed that takes seven rinses. It makes you throw up if you don't remove the sap. Don't save the water to make soup. Throw it away. After you are done with rinsing, the milkweed is an incredibly bright green. It is like cooking broccoli. It takes just a few minutes. I have eaten milkweed many times, and it is very good. It is sweeter than broccoli, which it resembles. Serve it like any vegetable, with butter on it. I've also had milkweed soup. My daughter loved it as a kid. My grandfather did not tell me about milkweed, but a lot of people we knew picked milkweed, because it is easy to find and easy to pick. Collecting several bags of it does not take long. It is tasty and free.

Picking these greens is not like picking blackberries, which means trips into the woods. Generally blackberries grow where bears live, and there are mosquitoes. All in all, the mosquitoes are worse than the bears. Wild strawberries come out just before mosquitoes, so they are easier to pick. Apples are easy to obtain, but asparagus and milkweed are easiest. They are not arduous to pick, and they are plentiful. Like asparagus, milkweed appears in groups. Bagfuls of it grow in one place.

Skunk cabbage is another food Menominees used as greens. Skunk cabbage is one of the very first things that comes up after winter, so its emerging leaves are a welcome sight. Gibbons talked about a way to make them palatable and edible. I think the plant is similar to spinach. It has that substance that puckers your mouth like spinach. I've been told that skunk cabbage, properly prepared, tastes like carob.

During the times when we would go out wild foraging, I ate plenty of dog roses. We boiled the tight, red rosebuds until they were soft. They were vegetables, really, that tasted like roses. Small rose leaves are good in salads, and ripened rose hips are like fruits. We waited until after the first hard frost when rosehips are soft and sweet and then ate them, after removing the seeds inside. We cut them open and scraped out seeds. The cleaned fruits were very sweet.

It wasn't that we needed the food so much as it was pleasurable to have an excuse to take a walk. Whenever we started to the door with gear, my small daughter would jump up. We would walk, look around, and observe the forest. One time we found a grove of fully ripe bing cherry trees. I had no idea they were growing in the nearby woodlands. We spent that afternoon gorging on cherries. After I taught my daughter how to pick dark as opposed to light fruit, her eyes got big, and she started stripping the branches she could reach. She had juice running down her face and clothes and a smiling face. She has a good diet to this day. One of the things her mother and I did right is provide her with a natural diet in her early years. One reason is simply that it was pleasurable to forage for fresh-picked food.

My grandparents were taught not to be Indians in their schooling. They were not really elders as far as knowledge of traditional plant foods. Take cranberries, for example. When we drove by the bog, Grandma would remember picking cranberries there, but that was when she was younger. She would say, Do you want to live in a tipi? Do you want to spend most of the day bringing wood home so you don't freeze to death? Yes, it sounds great, but do you want to do that? Do you want to chase a big animal with a spear? Grandmother did pick cranberries, but she chose what she would spend time on. She did not have time to gather fresh greens in the spring. She clerked at the family store from six-thirty a.m. to dark, so she depended on sauerkraut and other canned goods for our vegetables. Some Menominee families did keep up the traditional knowledge of plants. On the small reservation, the size of a county, a variety of traditions continued side by side with more modern practices.

After springtime greens come more plant seasons. Morels are an early mushroom, and other tree fungus and fungi were part of the traditional diet. Expert knowledge is needed to collect these, especially with climate change. Recently a cousin collected a poisonous variety new to the reservation area, almost identical to a food mushroom he had eaten all his life, and it was growing in the same spot. He came close to death.

Each tea or herb or root has a prime harvesting time. Herbs for medicinal use have the most potency just before flowering. Roots need a season to mature. As full summer arrives, most greens become tough and bitter. The new lime-green colors of fresh growth darken into solid primary green. Then it is time to forage for other foods.

Milkweed Cream Soup*

2 quarts of budded milkweed, picked just before blossoming
1 quart whole milk
½ cup flour
1 tablespoon butter or oil
½ cup cream
Salt and pepper to taste
½ pound diced cooked ham

Boil milkweed in 1½ quarts water until halfway cooked through, still firm. Drain. Repeat 3 or more times or until all bitterness is gone. Add the milk and heat through, without boiling or letting the milk stick. Mix some of the liquid into the flour, and then stir the flour into the soup. Add butter, cream, seasonings, and ham. Simmer until flavors meld.

*Some species of milkweed, like spider milkweed and whorled milkweed, are toxic. Common milkweed varieties may be eaten if boiled and drained and mature leaves, pods, stems, and seeds are avoided.

Sautéed Fiddlehead Ferns*

1 quart ostrich fiddlehead ferns (or cowslip greens)
4 slices bacon, cut into 1-inch pieces
½ teaspoon pepper

Clean and rinse the greens. Thin, papery scales cover new fiddleheads, and these need to be removed before cooking. Cut into 1-inch pieces. Boil in a small amount of water, or steam. In a skillet, cook the bacon. When fiddleheads are nearly cooked through, drain, then add to the skillet with bacon and cook until tender, about 5 minutes. Season with pepper.

*Only the ostrich fiddlehead fern (*Matteuccia struthiopteris*) is safe to eat. There is a deep U-shaped groove on the inside of the smooth stem. The end of the shoot curves into a spiral. Do not eat late-season fern fronds.

Dandelion Greens

2 quarts dandelion greens
1½ tablespoons butter or olive oil
Splash of vinegar
Salt and pepper to taste

Collect tender leaves before the plant blooms. Collect a large salad bowl's worth, about 2 quarts. Wash greens thoroughly, making sure to remove dirt and grit. Spin or pat dry. In a large stockpot on top of the stove, bring 2 quarts of water to a boil. Add greens. Cover and lower heat. Cook until tender, about 5 minutes. Drain through a colander and place in a serving bowl. Stir in butter, vinegar, and seasoning. Serve steaming hot.

Gardening

[The Menominees] always preserved seeds and carried them along with their traveling possessions, whatever they had. Seeds were encased in furhides, or dried and stored someplace where they knew they were coming back. Same way with products from the garden and dried meats, dried fish, dried fruits. They had it sewed up in bags, and covered with bark and buried these things where they knew they would come back at a later date. (Wescott, 2002)

My grandparents seldom used wild greens. They ate squash, green beans, cucumbers, radishes, and cabbages—all from their garden—but I cannot remember them eating salads. We had a large family, and the garden was a major source of food, cultivated under the direction of my grandfather. According to my grandmother's preferences, almost all garden produce was cooked until mushy soft. We ate bottles and bottles of pickles. Sauerkraut was a regular part of meals, and my mother continues to serve sauerkraut with pork and other meats. She pan-fried left-over sauerkraut for breakfast, and until I was an adult, I thought it was a Menominee food.

Grandma served potatoes at every meal. That was a staple from our garden that stored well. Grandpa liked the little red russets. We never had potato soup, though. We did not eat baked potatoes. My Aunt Lorraine once made twice-baked potatoes, as a novelty. My mother baked potatoes also, but my grandmother

cooked only fried potatoes, boiled potatoes, and mashed potatoes. Boiled potatoes with salt pork grease was good. Often bacon
drippings would suffice as seasoning. My aunts peeled a lot of
potatoes.

My grandfather had a farm between Zoar and Neopit, on a
straight line between the two. It was behind Camp Four Hill,
and behind Dutchman's Hill, a place beyond Dutchman's Field.
Having a farm on the Menominee reservation was possible that
far north. It's too far north for a complete growing season, but
in sheltered spots like this field, they were able to farm. There is
some incredibly rich soil, but it is only intermittent because it is
at the border of the Canadian Shield, granite bedrock. There are
no acres of contiguous good soil. Spots of good soil fit between
cracks and holes in the granite. The garden was in a wide space between blocks of granite. I remember being there as a small child.
This was not a truck farm, but the garden did produce enough
potatoes, corn, beans, and squash for most of the Weso clan.

From my teens onward, we lived in Keshena and were middle
class. Grandpa had salaried positions as game warden and justice of the peace. Because of his responsibilities, he did not have
time for hunting or fishing or gathering wild food. He chose not
to make time, either, but he did continue to garden. My grandmother enjoyed working at the store. She did not need to work,
since my grandfather had a salary. She liked it. This was during
World War II. She liked having her own money and indepen-
dence. Her generation of women, of the Depression and the war,
were more independent than the generation that followed.

My grandmother did not participate much in the garden, although many women did manage their family gardens and still
do. Menominee women may choose to hunt, fish, or garden
along with their other roles. Both women and men do beadwork.
Menominee people are a small, isolated group, and because of
this, perhaps, individuals have more choice, outside gender roles.

In my early teens, Grandpa moved our family garden to Uncle Bobby and Aunt Nita's part of the rez, Bear Trap Falls, the West Branch area. This plot was about forty by forty feet. By then, as he was in his fifties and sixties, he began using a rototiller. I remember he had a local farmer come in and disk it for the first time. This broke the virgin prairie, and after that, he needed only a rototiller.

Late into the autumn, we were still getting potatoes out of the ground. Grandfather would tend the garden at least a couple of hours a week. One of his favorite dishes was green beans with bacon. One year he gave my daughter, her mother, and me a large sack of cucumbers left over from the pickling process. For over a week, our daughter ate nothing but cucumbers and mother's milk. She was in diapers, but she loved the fresh, squishy food, and it did her no harm.

He did all that gardening, and it was his way of making sure all his extended family had food through the winter. He was tied to that garden. This was not a skill he learned at Haskell Institute, since my grandfather was a member of the US Army Indian Cavalry during his time there. This was during and after World War I. With his high school degree, he returned home to be a leader. Sometimes that meant long hours traveling among neighboring communities as a justice of the peace or game warden or spiritual leader. Sometimes it meant showing, through his garden, the natural laws of the plant world.

Baked Squash

3 acorn squash or other winter squash
3 tablespoons oil, butter, or drippings
Salt to taste
1 cup maple syrup

Wash and split squash lengthwise with a sharp knife. Remove seeds with a serrated knife or spoon. Save these to roast in the oven. Cut squash meat into 3-inch peeled pieces. Drizzle oil over the squash or dot with butter. Salt to taste. Add a coating of maple syrup to the shallow baking dish, at least an inch. Place squash in the syrup. Bake, covered, for 40 minutes at 350°F or until squash is tender. Remove and place on a serving dish. Pour remaining syrup over the squash.

To save time and use less syrup, cut squash in half, remove seeds, place meat side down in a half-inch of syrup, and bake as directed.

Pattypan Squash and Potato Boil

5 whole pattypan squash
8 Yukon Gold potatoes (or other thin-skinned variety,
    or 15 new potatoes)
4 tablespoons butter or oil (or olive oil, coconut oil,
    or bacon grease)
Salt and pepper to taste

Fill a large kettle with water and bring to a boil. While it is heating, scrub and clean the squash and potatoes. Peeling the potatoes is optional. When the water is heated, drop all the squash and potatoes into it. Keep at a full, rolling boil for 5 minutes, reduce heat to medium, and cover. Cook until tender, about 15 more minutes. Do not overcook, or the vegetables will be mushy. The squash skin will be tender after boiling. Drain through a colander. Put into a serving pan and dot with butter or oil. Add salt and pepper to taste.

Succotash

1 pint fresh green beans
4–5 ears fresh corn (or two 8-ounce packages frozen corn)
¾ cup whole milk or light cream

1 tablespoon butter or oil
Salt and pepper to taste

Wash and shell the green beans. This should result in about 8 ounces of tender green beans. Put beans in a saucepan. Discard the pods or save for vegetable broth. Cut corn from the ears using a sharp paring knife. To do this, brace the smaller end of the ear on a cutting board and shave the kernels off, saving the milk with the kernels. This should result in about 16 ounces of corn. Add these to the saucepan. Squeeze milk from the ears into the pan. Add milk, butter, salt, and pepper to the pan. Simmer slowly, stirring occasionally, until heated through, about 15 minutes. Do not overheat, or the milk will curdle.

Dried Pumpkin or Squash Seeds

2 cups raw pumpkin or squash seeds (saved when preparing
    other dishes)
1½ teaspoons salt
1 teaspoon soy sauce (or tamari or Worcestershire sauce),
    optional
1 tablespoon oil

Wash seeds thoroughly and remove stringy flesh. The drying process will make it easier to get the last flesh off the seeds. Toss the seeds with salt and soy sauce. Spread seeds so they are not touching on a lightly oiled baking sheet. Bake at 170°F for 3 hours or until the seeds are mostly dried out. Stir occasionally.

Blackberry Wine

*None of the chiefs would touch this mysterious firewater, so
three old men were selected to experiment. At first these reeled
and fell apparently dead, but, soon reviving, they told of
visions seen and delightful sensations experienced. Later doc-
uments will show clearly that the chiefs and people were more
than convinced of its desirability from then forward. It is often
referred to by the Indians as the "milk" given by the governor,
their parent, to his children; it came also to have an important
religious significance, as an aid in securing the all-important
dreams and visions. (Keesing, 1939)*

People still talk about Uncle Buddy on the Menominee rez. One
of the stories begins one spring when he bought six new garbage
cans. Nobody would buy something new in those cash-poor days
just to store trash. People waited for the garbage cans to fit into
a larger purpose.

On the rez everyone considered Buddy a leader—smart, brave,
loyal, educated. He was a flawed hero of World War II who returned from his last tour in Korea with a memory problem. He
could not forget the horrors of the white man's wars. In 1945 he had
spent months guarding German prisoners at Auschwitz. Before the
American public understood the existence of Nazi concentration
camps, he lived alongside the perpetrators. He saw immediately
and firsthand what they had done to the victims. People would
agree that Uncle Buddy had a pretty good reason to drink.

Enlisted men could buy hooch on credit, and in remote posts, if pressed, they could brew their own. During quiet times in the battlefields of Germany, Uncle Buddy learned the art of distillery. Before MREs, the enlisted men lived on potatoes, and these can make a passable vodka. He always called it hooch—a word that dates from just before Prohibition. It comes from a Tlingit word for any kind of potable alcohol. Buddy was smart and well-read, so he probably understood it was an Indian word.

I was a teenaged nephew, the oldest of the pack of nieces and nephews that Buddy babysat that summer. He ran a day care before the word was invented. He was a graduate student at the University of Wisconsin, on the GI Bill, and he took the summer off. His favorite wife had just left him. When he was truly in his cups, in that self-pitying state of a truly drunk man, he would tell me that Aunt Barbara was his one true love. He seldom got this intoxicated, as he had his maintenance level worked out by then. He never lacked for female company, but two or three times he descended the stairs into that subbasement-level drunkenness to weep about Barbara. The other women kept trying to fix him, but Barbara simply would not put up with him and left.

I was also a college student. I had been kicked out of the local school district, but according to Wisconsin law, I had to be in school. So at sixteen, I graced the steps of the Stevens Point campus, on occasion, and I enjoyed the college social life. At the end of the semester, I went home to the reservation and took up residence with the other outcasts, including Uncle Buddy, my mother's oldest brother. In Menominee tradition, the maternal uncle is a father.

As the warm days passed, I watched Uncle Buddy to see what he would do with the garbage cans. When the blackberries in the woods began to ripen, it became clear. Buddy talked to his brothers and sisters and encouraged them to send their offspring into his summer camp. Uncle knew he had a responsibility to the children as their oldest uncle, but he also knew how to turn situations to his advantage. Little kids never get tired of picking and eating blackberries. Over the next few weeks, the nieces and nephews trailed into the woods with baskets in hand and returned with mounds of blackberries. Another uncle taught them to look for blackberries by good trout streams. Somehow the two went together, and the older kids came back from excursions with fish ready to fry at the campfire. That fed the camp of half-grown children.

As one shiny garbage can was filled and then the next, the children were proud of their accomplishment. On rainy days, they sorted through berries and pulled out stray leaves and thorns. Children need tasks, Buddy said. He made it a game, and they enjoyed themselves while also giving their parents time to work at logging, fishing, or catching up on gossip. A few extra children were conceived during this interlude of free summer day care, while the little ones were exploring the woods.

I was reading Euell Gibbons's book *Stalking the Wild Asparagus*, and in the chapter on blackberries, I read about blackberry cordials and wine. I knew the neighboring Germans made blackberry schnapps and mixed it with pepper as a cure for diarrhea. Gibbons described the recipe for berry wine in detail, and I could see the procedure unfold through the next weeks: the picking, sorting, and fermenting.

The day came when Buddy decided the fragrant, purple mixture in the covered garbage cans was ready to drink.

"Nephew, it's done," he said. I could see he'd been sampling it already. The sink was filled with dirty dishes, and more were piled onto the kitchen table.

"I'm out of glasses," he apologized, "but let me pour you a bowl of hooch." He ladled the thick, purplish, sweetish, potent juice into two soup bowls, and we carried them carefully, sat down, and raised them to our mouths.

When that bowl was empty, he chanted, "More wine. More wine." He had taken a Greek history class and read *The Odyssey,* so he knew Greeks drank wine from bowls. He quoted as much as he could remember of the drunken scene, imitating Cyclops reeling and clutching the bronze spear in his one imaginary eye. By the end of the evening I had heard about Odysseus, the Trojan War, Menapus the Creator Rabbit, and much more. And then I slept.

With the project successfully completed, the children were dismissed from their duties and sent back to their parents. None was allowed to touch the wine.

People talked about the 330 gallons of blackberry wine for years afterward. The batch lasted the reservation the entire summer. As Buddy welcomed the most distant cousins who appeared for free hooch, we learned hospitality. It was a pleasant, mildly alcoholic drink that made even the grouchiest person relax. Veterans stayed late into the night and told war stories, and so I learned World War II history and its aftermath.

I admire Buddy's ability to organize almost thirty people—he could not have done this by himself. He knew the season's harvest was fleeting, he took advantage of it, he brought people together, and he enjoyed himself. That's the only time I saw my entire family of two hundred or so cousins get together outside of a funeral parlor.

Now I realize Buddy could have distilled 80-proof potato vodka if he were simply a drunk who needed to be inebriated. He had a greater plan in mind. He used this summer to get the young Menominees where they belonged, which was in the woods, not in front of television sets. That summer we learned chemistry and horticulture. We learned traditional medicine as well as the tribal lore Buddy taught.

When people tell stories about Uncle Buddy, like the time he hijacked the casino bus, there is always an aside to it, the knowing nod. He was crafty. That was a bit of his charm and a bit of his danger, too. He would go to great lengths to work out a con scheme, like bootleg hooch.

Maybe he represented Native culture in transition. He knew his father—my grandfather—was one of the last generation of traditional Indians, a true medicine man. Buddy knew he could not repeat the past. Buddy's was the generation that lost everything, including language and culture, and the white culture did not fit. However, Buddy was not like me, the most suburban Indian in the world. He was boxed in by these two generations, fore and aft, and did not fit into either. He did not embrace Christianity the way many people of his own generation did. He did not embrace farming. What he did was try to be an Indian. He was trying to establish a new culture. Sometimes that coincided with being a good citizen, and sometimes it did not. So there is an element of rebelliousness in that.

Finally, after the wine was gone, the story remains. That was Uncle Buddy's power, and maybe he foresaw it. Perhaps he knew that one day I would reflect on that summer. He made it memorable. He had "power" of a medicine family, but he never spoke about it directly, except to illustrate some story. Instead, he understood what power actually was and used it to everybody's betterment. That summer we all learned the essence of blackberries, their sweetness, and the consequences of excess. We learned the woods. We met distant relatives and heard about episodes in their lives. We heard about military hardships. Once Buddy, a paratrooper, was dropped over Panama with no way out. He ate lizards for six days, and he said they were not bad. He survived and found his way home.

When Europeans brought distilled spirits, they brought high-alcohol drinks that overwhelmed the senses. It was an endless, year-round supply. Worst of all, there was no ceremony to go with the feast. "Alcoholic" is a European concept created within the English language. The Menominee understanding would be drinking alcohol out of context of ceremony. In Peru the Incas still have a drinking ritual where the men and their llamas drink together. Then the ceremony comes to an end, like the summer-long supply of blackberry wine. While neighboring farmers drank fermented silage runoff year-round—it tastes like grass and is almost a hundred proof—we had a mild fruit wine brew. No fights broke out, although some serious romances started.

People liked Uncle Buddy, but not because he was lovable. He was a character and he was honest. He always kept his word, and he did things his own way. But he was not a lovable old character. You demean honored warriors by dismissing them as simply lovable.

Blackberry Wine

6 pounds blackberries
7 pints boiling water
2½ pounds granulated sugar
½ teaspoon pectic enzyme*
1 packet commercial wine yeast*
1 teaspoon yeast nutrient*

Wash berries and pick out stems, leaves, and bugs. Drain thoroughly in a colander. Place berries in a large kettle or crock, then mash with a potato masher. Pour boiling water over mashed blackberries. Allow to steep for two days, then strain through a fine-mesh sieve or cheesecloth. Add sugar to liquid and stir until it dissolves. Add pectic enzyme, cover well, and set aside for 24 hours. Add yeast and nutrient, cover, and set aside 5 to 6 days, stirring daily. Pour into dark glass bottles and fill to 2–3 inches from the top. Seal tightly. Save excess fluid for topping off. Store at room temperature, 70–75 degrees. After fermentation ends (foaming ceases), fill bottles to 1 inch of top. Store in a dark, 60- to 65-degree place for up to 3 months.

*Available from winemaking and home-brewing suppliers.

German Beer

*When they reached the Indian village, as soon as Turtle came
in sight of it, he sang at the top of his voice, "A warrior-hero/
Am I!/A warrior-hero/Am I!/Whoop!" were Turtle's words.
"Hey, what's happened to him? Why Turtle is drunk, Turtle
is drunk, Turtle is drunk!" said the people. And to be sure,
his hat was way to one side, like this, his hat, because he was
drunk. When they got to his wigwam, there was his brother.
"Hi, old boy, have a drink; I'm bringing some whiskey," he
said to his brother. So then his brother took a drink. "Oh,
thanks, Turtle," said his brother to him. To this day they are
said to have that barrel whiskey to drink; they are said to be
still drinking it. That is why Turtle does not run away when
one comes upon him anywhere. To this extent, it is said, he is
a warrior-hero. ("How Turtle Got Drunk," told by Nehtsiwi-
htuk, in Bloomfield,* Menomini Texts, 1928)*

My grandfather lived more than eighty years and hardly ever
took a drink. Some of his children did not do as well. It happens
with many families, with many cultures. I do not think that the
Menominee people drink any more or less than their German
neighbors in nearby towns. During my youth, my tribe was hard-
working, but cash poor. We simply could not, with our minimal
spending resources, support the hundreds of taverns surrounding
the reservation. German beer drinkers filled these places, but few
remember a drunken "white man." Many remember a drunken

"Indian." During that time, my grandfather socialized extensively with his German and Polish neighbors, talking over shared business. He always drank coffee.

I do not know if there really is dignity beyond death, but I know there is no dignity to being filled with alcohol. As a young child I would lie awake listening to the summer sounds of teenagers pulling into the reservation's only store in rumbling behemoths, before closing time at ten, to buy beer or cheap wine. Many mornings my grandparents would talk over the news of somebody's death, most of the time because of drunken driving. My grandfather spoke the Potawatomi dialect of Algonquin, while my grandmother spoke Menominee, but all of us children could translate enough to make sense of their conversations. Besides, they would look meaningfully at one of my uncles or aunts, and that would be enough. Yet the next day there would be many drinks lofted for the fallen youth. Pain begets pain.

There is a traditional Menominee story about Turtle getting drunk. He is a trapper in the story, and after a hard winter killing beaver, he takes the huge load of furs to the trader. Part of his spoils, besides a new suit, is a barrel of whiskey. But the whiskey makes him act ridiculous, and people make fun of him. To this day Turtle is slow because of that barrel of whiskey he drinks from. Grandpa told me of the times the white people from town would get some Indian drunk, like foolish Turtle. Sometimes this was done forcibly. For many years we avoided the nearby reservation border town, Gresham, Wisconsin, because of its reputation of such actions against Menominees. When I got my first car, I drove to Gresham to see if the white people still did this. I was left alone.

Drunken driving killed many of my people. Cheap entertainment was to go into town and view the latest car wrecks, displayed for the general public, at the local garage. This was between the Dairy Queen and the reservation. We ate our treats while slowing

down to see the effects of carnage. Sometimes older people became casualties. I lost an uncle and an aunt on my birthday to a
drunk driver. Teens, cars, and alcohol make a deadly cocktail in
any culture.

Vietnam killed many Menominee men of my generation, and
more died indirectly through substance abuse. Because we had
grown up without hope, the army found us to be easy recruits. In
high school, for non-Menominees on the college track, Latin was
the required foreign language. My friends and I were working-
class Indians, and we were taught French. The school thought they
were doing us a favor by teaching us a language for the army, even
though it was no longer spoken in Vietnam. With no skills except
French and woodworking, we went straight to the front lines.

Returning Vietnam vets found their home had not changed,
but they had. Hard and serious drugs entered our reservation,
through people who had become used to killing and who did not
hesitate to do so again. I grew old with the smell of late-afternoon
funerals and the sound of women crying. Native people have
the highest rate of participation in the military. Now veterans,
men and women, return from Iraq, Afghanistan, and other wars.
Some have lost limbs; some have mental scars. The Menominee
Nation in Wisconsin funds Maehnowesekiyah Wellness Center
to support healthy recovery.

Alcohol can be a gentle companion to meals and conversa-
tion. It can be a poison with a steep mortality rate.

Dandelion Wine
(Mrs. Paul Dodge, Keshena, Wisconsin, *Indian Cook Book:
Menominee County Womans Club*)

2 quarts dandelion flowers (yellow fuzz only)
¾ gallon boiling water
½ cup raisins

Juice of 3 lemons
Juice of 2 oranges
3 pounds granulated sugar
1 package cake yeast

Collect a large salad bowl's worth of mature dandelion fuzz, about 2 quarts. Steep dandelions in boiling water and let stand 24 hours, then strain, reserving liquid. Add raisins to strained liquid, plus lemon and orange juice, sugar, and yeast. Let stand for at least 9 days, then strain and put in bottles, but do not seal for 45 days.

Rose Hip Tea

3 tablespoons dried rose hips
1 quart boiling water

Collect ripe rose hips after the first frost. If you wait for hips to dry on the bushes, they may lose flavor. Here is a way to control this by drying them in the kitchen. Wash thoroughly and drain. Pick out leaves and stems. Spread on a cookie sheet and place in a warm oven, 200°, for 4 hours or until rose hips turn dark red. Remove bud ends, crush, and store in a cool, dry place.

To make tea, put rose hips in a tight mesh tea strainer. Pour boiling water over the rose hips and allow to steep for 10 minutes. Sweeten the tea to taste. Some old recipes suggest adding dried orange peel for extra flavoring. Wintergreen leaves also can be used to make a crisp-tasting tea.

Wisconsin Diner Food

Beefsteak Toast. Chop cold steak very fine, cook in a little
water, put in cream or milk, thicken, season with butter,
salt, and pepper, and pour it over slices of toast. Prepare
boiled ham in the same way, adding the yolk of an egg.
(*Gortner, in* Buckeye Cookery and Practical Housekeeping: Compiled from Original Recipes, 1877)

My grandfather did not go to McDonald's. He would go to Cul-
ver's, which in Wisconsin is a fast-food joint with hamburgers
made of real beef, not pink slime, and frozen custard. He did enjoy
A&W root beer, but not their hamburgers. Not in a million years
would he go to a chop suey joint, as he called Chinese restaurants.
Neither he nor my grandmother would go to any kind of ethnic
restaurant, nor did they ever try fine dining. The story goes that a
white visitor came to visit my grandparents with a bottle of wine
and some T-bone steaks. My grandfather had never had wine or
a T-bone steak. They did not even own a corkscrew. My grandmother ended up throwing the steaks in the oven and baking
them until very well done and a uniform gray. All our meat was
fried or baked. My grandparents were very traditional Indians.

Let me explain further. Once I was watching a show about
British chefs who were visiting the Seminoles in Florida. Each
chef was trying to create fine dining out of Florida swamp ingredients. One did something with alligator. The Seminole Indians
said nothing. One tried cooking fresh oysters, but no response.

Finally, one of the British chefs fried a garpike in a pan of grease. The Seminole Indians said, "Oh, that one is cooked right." This is not a socioeconomic issue, but a cultural one.

One more story. On a television documentary, a white anthropologist visited an Aboriginal group in Australia. He goes out with a local fisherman, both of them outfitted with fishing spears. The Aborigine gets a big stingray, drags it up to shore, grabs a bludgeon, and beats it for twenty minutes from every angle. He then throws the bloody carcass on the fire. In the meantime, the anthropologist catches a shark, cuts a steak from it, and then grills it on the fire. The Aborigine pulls the stingray off the fire, cuts it open, reaches inside, grabs the pulverized stingray flesh, and eats it with relish. When the shark is barely cooked through, the anthropologist starts to eat it. The Aborigine says something, and the subtitled English is: "Boy, these white guys will eat anything." What is a delicacy to one is abhorrent to the other.

My grandparents were no exception to cultural preferences. My grandmother would be horrified to know I eat eel in sushi. While it wasn't taboo—no food is taboo to the Menominee—it just wasn't part of our food culture. Eel is one of the foods our tribe seldom ate. I do not remember my grandparents ever eating mutton or lamb. When I lived with them, we had beef and pork, but not for every meal. We had meat every meal, but it was usually wild game and fish. There are ways that a Menominee cook prepares all of these, and Grandma did not stray outside these recipes. In the example of the fried gar and the Seminoles, I doubt Seminoles would eat gar sushi. It simply is not their cultural idea.

My grandfather was open to many ideas and was a little vain. He did care what others thought of him, and he wanted to appear sophisticated. Later in life, Grandpa would have a glass or two of wine. He did not initiate it, but sometimes he was served wine and he did not refuse it.

Though he disliked most fast food, my grandfather did like diners, in the traditional Wisconsin style: the neighborhood kitchens. Today the word *diner* evokes the greasy spoons found in 1950s film noir. Wisconsin diners were different, more often places that served hearty comfort food. Diners connected the people in the area, Indians, Germans, and Poles. In Wisconsin it was very common to have Friday night fish fries, since the default religion for just about everybody was Catholic. Coleslaw, rye bread, a chunk of butter, walleye—these were the expectation. Perch was another fish for Friday fish fries. Sometimes people brought my grandparents Friday night carryout so they would not have to go to the taverns with beer drinkers. Sometimes we would go out.

Generally, we ate at diners when we traveled to fairs and prayer meetings at an Indian church. Sometimes we would travel to Appleton or Milwaukee to visit a museum. We traded stories with other Menominee families about which diners were friendly to Indian customers and which were not.

Wherever we went, Grandpa liked one item in particular, a hot roast beef sandwich. One place in Antigo, right on Main Street, fixed it perfectly. I wonder about the origins of the hot roast beef sandwich, where it came from before it became a staple of Wisconsin diners. An 1877 cookbook from Indiana describes "beefsteak toast," made from diced, cooked beef, served with gravy over toast. It was seasoned with butter, salt, and pepper. This was about the same as the diner chefs fixed, except soft white bread, not toast, sops up the gravy more completely. This working-class meal uses leftovers effectively for either diners or home cooks. Stale bread and cold meat from the previous day transform into this comfort food dish.

I have never been to any diner where the restaurant owner buys a beef roast, cooks it slowly, slices it thin, and then covers it with gravy. Almost always, the meat is presliced, precooked beef, prepared for the restaurant business by Sysco Foods in Baraboo. An Arby's roast beef sandwich is freshly cooked, which is their selling point. They have a chunk of meat in the back that they cook and then slice. At the small diner in Antigo, however, the cooks did not even slice their own meat. They merely assembled the meal. The gravy, probably canned, went over the beef and two slices of white sandwich bread. My grandparents both liked white bread better than whole wheat. They thought that refined food was more civilized. Colonization did not offer better solutions, only different solutions.

Always, the Wisconsin short-order cooks served mashed potatoes with the open-faced beef sandwich, and the mashed potatoes were instant. My grandmother liked instant better, because they were more uniform. The fiber and starch were removed to make a more symmetrical texture that could be scooped perfectly. The diner used an ice cream scoop to create a sphere of pasty white potatoes. The taste was slightly different from that of real mashed potatoes. Potatoes were a major crop in the area, so I wonder at the preference for the packaged version.

Canned corn on the side finished the hot roast beef meal. I am sure that if my grandfather were here and we served beef Wellington, he would not eat it. It would be too different. If it were rare, he would say, "Tommy, it's not even cooked. There's blood coming out of it." I ate many hot roast beef sandwich meals with my grandfather, and sometimes on the road I order them to remember how much he loved them.

Diner Fish Fry

3 fresh perch or other small fish, cleaned and halved
2 eggs
½ cup milk
½ cup flour

½ cup crushed Saltine crackers, rolled fine
1 teaspoon baking powder
1 teaspoon salt
½ teaspoon pepper
2 tablespoons shortening (or more as needed)

At the diner, use the deep fat fryer filled with fresh shortening. At home, use shortening, melted in a deep-sided frying
pan. Wash and pat dry the fish pieces. Set aside. Beat eggs and
gradually add milk. Pour into a shallow pan, such as a 9-inch
pie pan, for dipping. In another bowl or pan, mix flour, cracker
crumbs, baking powder, salt and pepper. Heat shortening on
medium high until it sizzles when a drop of water touches it.
Roll fish pieces in the flour-cracker mixture and then the egg
mixture. Roll again in the flour mixture. Carefully drop fish
pieces into the frying pan. Cook on one side until the coating
is crispy, 4–5 minutes. Turn over with tongs and cook until
the coating is cooked through and the fish flakes with a fork,
about 3 minutes longer. Remove and serve immediately.

Pickled Pig's Feet

6 fresh pigs' feet, split in half lengthwise
2 quarts or more white vinegar
1 medium onion, chopped
2 bay leaves
2 tablespoons salt
½ tablespoon mustard seed
1 teaspoon peppercorns

Wash pigs' feet thoroughly and singe off hair. Place in a large
pot, adding enough water to cover. Bring water to a boil over
medium-high heat. Reduce heat to a simmer and cook until
tender, about 1 to 1½ hours. Stir occasionally, skimming off

any foam. Remove cooked pigs' feet and rinse in scalding water. Remove as many bones as possible. Wash the pot, then add 2 quarts vinegar, or enough to fill the pot two-thirds full. Add onion and seasonings. Bring vinegar mixture to a boil, reduce heat, and simmer for about 30 minutes. Add pigs' feet back in. Bring to a full boil, then turn off heat. Remove the feet and pack in clean jars with vinegar solution to within ½ inch from the top. Screw the cap tight. Process jars in water bath for 90 minutes. Cool slowly. Refrigerate sealed jars for 3 to 7 days before eating.

Fair Time on the Rez

Indian Fair—The Menominee Indians, in imitation of their
white brothers, held a fair at Keshena last Monday. A large
number of our citizens attended, and all expressed aston-
ishment at seeing the large amount of vegetables displayed,
consisting of several varieties of potatoes, turnips, beets, car-
rots, radishes, squashes, corn, etc. There was quite a display
of needle-work by the [women] of the tribe. The premiums
awarded amounted to about $140. Mr. Maurer, of this city,
delivered the address, which was interpreted to the Indians
by Joseph Gauthier. Mr. Maurer gave them many valuable
suggestions, which we hope they will remember. Many of the
Indians, during the last two years, have settled down and
gone to farming, and have good farms under cultivation.
(Shawano County Journal, *12 September 1874*)

Fair time was a time for the Menominee community to come
together. In my early childhood in the 1950s, I remember fairs
at the white community of Shawano, Wisconsin, and also the
fair on my reservation, where my grandparents ran a concession
stand. Late at night, after the rides closed down, the men would
get together and talk past midnight. I miss the calliope of noise
and smells and sights.

At the Shawano fair, near the rez, the 4-H clubs displayed
fruits of their efforts, including prize cattle, pigs, and poultry. A
highlight was stock car racing, as well as carnival rides run by

Belle City Amusements, still a major carnival company. At food stands, fairgoers could buy cream puffs, brats, and beer. This was a meeting place for members of the opposite sex, important to me as a young teenager. This fair continues to be an anticipated event for the region's white farmers, with tractor pulls and a dog show.

The Menominee tribe had a fair in Menominee County at the reservation as early as 1874, when the Shawano newspaper mentions it. It included crop displays as well as beadwork. The Menominee fair in Keshena seemed eternal to me as a young boy. I used to nose around the fairgrounds—my grandmother called my ramblings "nosing around"—and at that time there were several very old, dilapidated buildings, now torn down, that may have been from the nineteenth century. One was a barn for cattle and horses. At one time, there were enough farmers on the reservation to display livestock as white people did. Today, the main industry on the rez is log milling and the casino, not raising livestock.

During my time, there were still typical fair events at the Menominee fairgrounds, like the women's canning competition for applesauce, jellies, jams, pickled apples, and so forth. Menominees added their own twist to European American customs. There were horse races. We had some cousins, the Wynos family, who raced small ponies. They did not win money for racing, but they made side bets. This was a holdover from the Indian tradition of gambling, and casinos are a new manifestation.

My grandparents had a concession stand on the fairgrounds as one of their seasonal occupations. I don't know what legal relationship they entered into with the tribe to do this, but this was an important part of our family's summer income. I was really young the first year our family had the stand. Several weeks before fair time, Rodney (my stepfather), Uncle Buddy, my grandfather, and Uncle Bobby dug a septic tank underneath our site, so we had a sink in the concession stand. We put a new roof on the building we occupied as well. The stand was about twenty feet by twenty feet, with shuttered windows on the sides. The building was divided into three parts, to accommodate storage, a kitchen area, a hallway, and a serving area. We sold a lot of cigarettes and beer, so we stored these in the back room. My grandmother was forever cleaning and directing my aunts to clean.

Because people started arriving days before the fair, my grandparents and the extended family were there a week beforehand to get ready. They started selling basic foods three days before the fair, and we served hot food starting two days before the fair, because Indians would show up early for a powwow that took place at the same time as the fair near the current site of the Woodland Bowl, a natural amphitheater. This is where the Menominee Powwow still occurs annually, first weekend of August. Back then, people would put tarps over existing wigwam frames and camp. Indian people danced in a powwow behind a stockade fence, and they charged money to get in. Later photographs show a corral-like fence, but this stockade fence was solid. It is no longer there.

Carnival people began arriving several days early, too, including the Dusty Rhodes show. Rhodes was a professional wrestler, but from the 1940s to 1962 he and his wife, Edith, toured the Rhodes Rides Carnival. He played the Keshena fair and similar-sized fairs throughout the upper Midwest during the summer, and then he wintered in Florida.

My grandmother was famous for her meat pies, baked beans, and chili. The meat pies were not a fast-selling item, but not because they weren't popular. My grandmother would not tell everyone she had meat pies, but some people she would let know, and they would get a big chunk of it with homegrown green beans, bread, and butter. My sister made me a meat pie recently with a flaky crust and a filling of gravy and meat—no added vegetables. This was like the meat pies of my grandmother.

Grandma's baked beans were a customer favorite. For the fair, she had a huge roaster filled with beans, slow cooked with real ham, not pork hocks. She did not bake the beans, but rather depended on slow cooking to soften the beans and meld the flavors. The beans were dark and rich, with molasses, tomato sauce, and well-cured ham. These are mythic in my memory. At home, she would make egg salad with fry bread, and serve these with her baked beans. Grandma did not make a lot of fry bread, but this was one of my grandfather's favorite meals. She made the egg salad with real mayonnaise, dill pickles (not sweet), and diced hardboiled eggs.

At the fair, other organizations like the Veterans of Foreign Wars had concession stands, as did a few other families. Most stands sold beer and burgers or brats. One served fried chicken and egg salad. Grandma served hot dogs but not brats, since these were available at other stands. Her mainstay was full meals. People would stay at the fair all day and into the night, and they got tired of hamburgers and soda. Friday night would go by, then Saturday was when people would bring the kids early for the cheaper prices on rides. They needed a hot meal by the end of the day.

Either my grandfather or my grandmother slept nights in the stand with my uncles, to guard it. The kids and everyone else slept at our house in nearby Keshena. That group would arrive at the fairgrounds by five a.m., partly to take advantage of business, and also because there were so many of us in the family for breakfast. We raised the windows and sat on benches outside, where there was room. My grandmother made bacon, eggs, toast, and coffee. As she fed her family, assisted by her daughters, she made enough for the fair workers, too. That early in the far north, it was getting light by five, and work at the fair was almost around the clock. All the white guys working at the fair ate at my grandmother's because she had the best food. She was always very clean as well, and my aunts were always scrubbing down the kitchen and doing dishes. Grandma had a bigger variety of food on offer than other stands, too.

My grandmother was more than a competent cook. Her talent was the ability to use available foods and maximize the taste and depth of flavor. Her dishes were simple but well cooked. She did not take any shortcuts. Chili was an example of this. Everybody made chili from mostly the same ingredients, but hers was better. For the fair, she always used ground beef, but at home, this was a dish that helped use up venison, not a family favorite. She ground the tougher, gamier venison and seasoned it with chili powder from a can. It had no peppers in it, no fresh tomatoes. She used the same chili powder as everybody else, the same beef, the same canned tomatoes, and no beans. What was different? Maybe she did like my aunt does and added a cup of lard. This sounds horrible today, but if you are working in the woods or do anything in the cold, you need grease and calories. My grandmother never cooked with pasta, so she did not add macaroni as is in many northern chili recipes.

Fair time meant lots of bottled beer. We sold beer as soon as we opened in the morning, sometimes five a.m. By late Saturday night, everyone was drinking, except my grandparents and a few others. Those who did drink made up for the others. Late one Saturday night, we children and our minders were going back to my grandparents' house. We were all packed in the car when we hit a big traffic jam at the Keshena highway bridge. The road was down to one lane because of an accident up ahead. Finally, it was our turn. We looked down and saw this very drunk guy with his head caught in the steel girder bridge, roaring and struggling. I heard people talking about how he had been slamming beers at the fairgrounds, and now he got himself into this mess. The fire department had to get him out. Everyone was looking and laughing. He was a good object lesson for us children.

A mix of neighboring German and Polish people came to the fair as well as tribal peoples—Mole Lake Ojibwe and Forest Band Potawatomi, especially. The Menominee tribe did not officially exist at this time, because of federal termination policies, but we thought of ourselves as a tribal nation. We were different from the many Legend Lakers there at the time. These were white people who took over the former Menominee ricing beds. By damming the stream and building a golf course nearby, they destroyed the ecosystem of Legend Lake. Still, they were neighbors, and many attended our events. It was not unusual to see white people during powwow times, especially Saturday night when the Woodland Bowl was alive with singing and drumming.

We used to go to a lot of lumberjack breakfasts in white communities around the rez. Churches sponsored some of these events, or sometimes fire departments. One of the entertainments was to suspend a keg of beer on a wire overhead. Firefighters would squirt hoses at it, and whoever got the keg to their side won the keg. This spectacle entertained the crowd and raised money. The breakfast was sausage links, eggs, pancakes, oatmeal, maple syrup, applesauce, cherries, coffee, and toast. I loved cinnamon toast with raisins. This may sound like a lot of food, but for workers, white or Menominee, long hikes to work were the norm, a mile or more into the forest carrying a chainsaw, an axe, and a gun. None of these is light. At these meals I ate a tall stack of pancakes, half a tub of butter, and lots of maple syrup. We didn't have biscuits and gravy, but this was hearty fare for all the people who lived in the Great White North.

Photographs taken by Harmon Percy Marable between 1911 and 1920 show pony races, a carousel, a Ferris wheel, and a parade at the Menominee fair, as well as powwow dancers. I remember these, and also the Tilt-a-Whirl. The Menominee fair lasted from the 1870s throughout my childhood in the 1960s and beyond. Sometime in the 1970s, the tribal powwow became the dominant celebration, and the abandoned fair buildings fell into disrepair. These days, every first weekend of August, concession stands set up early for the annual tribal powwow. They feed streams of powwow dancers and visitors. People still get together to talk and renew community ties, and meals always are at the center of these gatherings.

Baked Beans

1 pound small dried beans, such as great northern, navy, or pinto beans, picked over and rinsed
8 ounces diced ham
3 cups water
1½ cups ketchup
⅔ cup maple sugar
¼ cup molasses
2 tablespoons salt
2 tablespoons yellow mustard
1 tablespoon apple cider vinegar

Soak beans overnight in salted water and rinse. In a Dutch oven or roaster, brown the diced ham. Add rinsed beans and 3 cups water. Bring to a boil, then lower heat. Stir in the remaining ingredients. Cook, covered, on medium low until tender, about 4 hours. Remove lid and cook another hour, until thickened.

Chili

2 pounds of ground venison or beef, or a mixture of the two
½ to 1 cup lard
1 onion, diced
2–4 bell, jalapeño, poblano, or other peppers, diced (optional)
2 (4-ounce) cans tomato paste
2 (16-ounce) cans diced tomatoes
3 tablespoons chili powder

1 tablespoon brown sugar

1 tablespoon salt

1½ teaspoons black pepper

Brown the meat in the lard. Set meat aside, leaving drippings in the pan. Brown a diced onion in the drippings. Add diced fresh peppers if desired. Add tomato paste and diced tomatoes. Bring to a boil and reduce heat. Mix meat into the onions and tomatoes, and add seasonings and brown sugar. Simmer on medium low for 1 to 2 hours.

Storage

Winters preserved foods naturally. The cold springs that dot the reservation were year-round coolants. [Paul Hawpetoss] used a box with several 1-inch holes in each end and set it in the little stream that flowed from the spring, so that the water ran through the holes in the box. In the bottom were several large flat stones to hold it down and to set the dishes of food on. The stones held the chill of the water, and that box was almost as cool as a regular refrigerator. It was in the shade of a big pine, so that the sun never hit it. The lid was held down by a heavy stone, so that small animals couldn't get at his provisions. (Norick, 1980)

In the 1950s at my grandparents' house on the Menominee reservation, we were feeding at least a dozen, sometimes two dozen people. Long-range planning was absolutely essential to keeping everybody fed. Grandma kept my uncles busy, not so much with the actual hunting and fishing, but organizing them to arrive home at appropriate times with that larder. My aunts were always busy in the kitchen, under her direction, as sous chefs. Storage of meat, garden produce, maple syrup, wild rice or *manomin*, milk, and store-bought goods was essential. Grandma had a place for everything, from the outbuildings to the eaves to the basement. Each part of their houses adapted to storage of food. The houses also had room for stored spirits, the ghosts.

The first house that I remember had long, narrow, and steep stairways. It had been owned by a white minister at one time. That was in Zoar, Wisconsin, at the northwestern edge of the reservation. From the third floor of that house, I once jumped down those stairs thinking that I could fly. I can remember being airborne one moment, then blackness.

The house seemed old, even then. I remember photographs of myself and my brother in the front yard. These are yellowed and dog-eared images from the olden days. Several pictures show me sitting on top of a horse in the front yard dressed as a cowboy, toy guns strapped to my waist. I was told by Uncle Buddy that these were Hopalong Cassidy six-shooters. I never asked Uncle Buddy how he knew this. It is probable that he bought them for me. Uncle Buddy was not a touchy-feely person. In fact, most people were afraid of him, because Buddy had a temper and some very definite ideas about propriety. But Uncle Buddy was the closest thing to a father that I ever had. It was not until I had moved to Kansas in my forties and married a Kansan that I dressed like a cowboy again—cowboy hat, boots, and a pearl-button shirt. The garb brought back warm feelings about my uncle. I barely remember the house, but the photographs renew my imagination.

I loved my grandparents' next house, and this one I remember foremost as the great storehouse of food. This house in Keshena had been built by the Indian Service as an administration building. There were, and still are, plenty of Indians in the northern third of Wisconsin, and the government needed a headquarters. It was soundly built, and later it was converted into a jail. My grandparents bought it in the late 1950s, some years after my birth in 1953.

The building was a Gothic-style red brick building. It was an architectural reflection of the Jesuit school and convent a quarter of a mile away on top of the hill. These three buildings were gloomy and reminiscent of European superstition. They must have been built by the same architect. Only our old house—rather, the skeleton of our old house—still sits along the Wolf River floodplain. The convent and the Jesuit school are long since gone, barely remembered by me and forgotten by the more mentally healthy townsfolk.

I remember each room of that house. Just outside the coal room, in the kitchen pantry area, Uncle Donny built some shelves. These were filled with canned fruits. We had the usual assortment of applesauce, spiced apples, and apple butter, but we also had canned blackberries, canned raspberries, canned cherries, and canned hull corn, which is a northern Indian posole corn.

There were also many quarts of maple syrup that we made ourselves. The women in the family canned quarts of the finished syrup. Grandpa loved maple sugar cakes, a final finished product. These maple sugar cakes were hung in the cool, dry coal room. Those would get eaten quickly.

That old house stored more than food. Everyone who lived there experienced its ample supply of ghosts. Its previous existence as a jailhouse contributed to its status. My grandmother once spent a night in that house when it was a jail. She became overly demonstrative at a tribal meeting. Threatened with contempt, she wouldn't stop her accusations of corruption against the Indian Service. Grandpa never let her forget it. Her cell was to become one of our upstairs bedrooms.

Unsurprisingly, this building was haunted with the afterimages of thieves, drunks, brawlers, and a few murderers, and something else. Upstairs, there were shadow people dancing without melody along the walls—passing through walls, continuing their dance from room to room. They did not frighten me, not even as a child. They were my playmates as they danced on all four walls of my bedroom. They did, however, frighten my aunts. Later I was told by all three that they had never spent time in that house by

themselves, and never overnight. I stayed in the house and slept
the nights away by myself plenty of times. In fact, only Grandpa,
Uncle Buddy, and I ever spent the night there alone.

Still, even I never went downstairs to the basement-level
kitchen by myself after dark. There was something very bad that
stirred in the darkness that during the day lived behind, or maybe
within, our giant coal-fired boiler. Around ten at night—and it
was always around ten at night—something would gather its
strength and make its way upstairs. I could hear it turn on the
lights as it crept up the cement steps.

The light switches were those old-timey kind, spring-loaded
so they would turn on or off with a distinctive loud snap. Many
times at night I could hear those switches snap on and off. I do
not know why this happened. It might be that there were several
of them, the entities, not just one. If I was really quiet, I could hear
this thing come into the main house, moving through the furnace
room. I did not hear footsteps, exactly, but I could sense a stride.
Past the kitchen, past the wall where all the light switches were
located, then snap, the light switches would make their distinctive
loud sound, past the spot where fifty years later my Uncle Buddy
would be murdered. Then up the stairs, slowly, delicately, like
a cat, or better yet, like a malevolent wolverine, what the local
whites call the hodag.

Sometimes, so frightened that I could barely see, I would head
toward the landing, to where I could look over the stairs, to deter-
mine if the lights were really turned on—to prove an existence,
or nonexistence, once and for all. Just before reaching that point
where I could actually see, the light switches would snap back
off. After a while, I wouldn't bother to look anymore. I still would
hear the switches from under the covers in my bed. I still sensed a
presence. It would get very dark in the stairway, not just dim, but a
darkness that was devoid of all light. Something even darker came
up the stairs. It always took its time. Perhaps it knew that it got

scarier the longer that it took, or maybe, perhaps, it was old, much older than my grandparents. It would momentarily linger at each step. The being would tarry on the landing, as though it stopped to look outside through the only window in the hallway, a small window facing the driveway. This window, left over from the jail years, was mounted in the stout door where prisoners marched in. This dark entity returned often during my childhood years as I tried to sleep in the old block of cells.

One time, in a warm summer's daylight, I walked up the driveway to that door, to enter my home. Just as I reached the door, the curtain on the door was pushed aside, and an ancient and tired woman looked out the window at me with unblinking eyes. That was the only time that I was too frightened to go inside the house. I turned around and went to Shawano and spent the night with a friend. I knew then, as I know now, that it was not the ghost of some prisoner doomed to reenact a tragedy from its past. Then as now, I'm sure that whatever it was, it was never alive, not alive with human life, anyway. This was not death. Death is not the opposite of life. When we die, we shift to another existence. This was negative life—alive with nonlife. That's the only way to describe it.

While my aunts saw, felt, and heard many things in that house, I think that I was the only one to experience that thing coming up the stairs. When I moved away, that thing, or maybe it was better described as a nonthing, moved with me. It was only about five years ago that it finally got tired of Lawrence, Kansas, and moved on to torment somebody else. Yes, sleeping there in my grandparents' house by myself was creepy, but I did stay there by myself many times. This was my home for many years, and I thought that everybody had a haunted house. For me that was normal. Besides, I was a Menominee and all Menominee people know that sometimes the dark things from our nightmares walk the same paths that we do. So storage in our house included upkeep of these entities. We never worried about the spirits getting into the canned food, but they had their own appetites. They wanted us to acknowledge them.

Every room in that house had some kind of spirit clinging to it. My grandfather was one of the last of the real Indians, a medicine man, or perhaps a witch. I think that was why we came to have that collection of nighttime shadowy beings. It was through my grandfather's magic that these things lived, or experienced life. They did not frighten him, but they enjoyed frightening the rest of the family. Perhaps that was how they gained energy, how they "ate."

The room from where all nonlife came was itself quiet. Only the furnace room was not haunted. That one room that was filled with the essence of my grandfather, who was a loving, accepting, and tolerant man. It gets cold in that part of Wisconsin, and without heat, people freeze to death. We had a giant coal-burning boiler in the furnace room. One of my jobs was to feed shovelful after shovelful of coal into the boiler, and then the furnace would come to life. With a whoosh, I could feel the heat coming in, wave after wave. The room just opposite the furnace was devoted to the storage of coal. That stockpile was as crucial to life as food stored in the larder.

I can remember giant dump trucks filled with black coal, backing toward the house, getting closer and closer before stopping. There was a small door on the side of the house. My grandparents kept that small door locked from the inside. When the coal trucks arrived, it was my job to run downstairs, then scamper across the diminished leftover mounds of coal and turn that lock.

I enjoyed watching the coal delivery from the coal room. The truck driver pushed a long metal tray through the opening, and soon I could hear the truck raise its bed. Then, slowly at first but picking up speed, coal would begin to rain down, a dust cloud filling the room. The room was fifteen by twenty by ten feet. I do not know how much coal could fit inside, but there was a lot of coal, big chunks of soft black rocks.

In the summer we did not use the furnace. In the coal room, the leftover coal was swept into a corner, and the room became a storage room for food. In one corner were huge bags of potatoes, several hundred pounds. We also stored squash in the coal room. My job was to sort and stack the squash. Winter squash, Hubbard and acorn varieties, went on one side of the room. On the other side of the room we kept summer squash. The bright green, soft-shelled squash was just perfect for boiling with a bit of salt pork for flavoring.

Although my grandfather did not hunt, many people would stop over and give us chunks of venison. Grandma would dry it and grind it into a fine powder. We would eat handfuls of it. She would add it to soups. That had a place in the storage room. We also had bags of dried corn hanging from the ceiling. Again, my grandmother would dry the corn and grind it into powder.

My grandfather told me that when coal cost four dollars a ton, he thought it was much too expensive, so he decided to switch to using wood for heat. From that point on, the coal room became his workroom. He kept some power tools there and sometimes worked on art projects. To me, though, this room became the space that I loved best in the house, to sit inside and be safe.

Many years later, and just after my Uncle Buddy's murder, the old coal-fired furnace was considered too inefficient, too wasteful, and it was finally removed. It was much too big to fit through any of the doors. When our house was under construction, this furnace was brought by freight wagon to Keshena, Wisconsin, mounted upon the foundation floor, and then the house was built around it. To remove it, several men with blowtorches went to work cutting it into small pieces. These pieces were carried out the back door and respectively placed, like an honored dead Menominee, on a big truck. Fire is sacred in all its forms. This behemoth was taken to a recycling site to become other bits and pieces of Americana. With the furnace gone, silence characterized my childhood home for perhaps the first time.

As an adult, I explored the furnace room again. For several hours I sat there. I looked at where the furnace used to sit from every angle in the room. I discovered another old window, long since covered in brick and mortar. Perhaps this window marked the original coal chute. I never saw any trace of evil in the room. Maybe the dark being once lived in the old furnace. Maybe it ate coal and was hungry when we switched to wood. Maybe it used the furnace to hide, and maybe I am a relative of that evil thing. I am one of the few family members still alive out of all the people that lived in that Keshena house with that old furnace, the light switches that turned on and off, and a presence that came out of hiding when it was dark.

Since then, I have never gone back to that house, my home of haunted memories. Now they are stored within me. I still have a taste for boiled squash and potatoes. I use wild rice, salt, water, and maple syrup every way possible.

Dried Corn

6 to 8 ears of corn, or 3 (8-ounce) packages frozen corn

Cook corn on the cob and remove kernels, or buy good-quality canned or frozen corn. Rinse and drain well. Pat dry. Spread on baking sheets so kernels do not touch each other. Roast in slow oven, about 200°F, for 4 hours or until kernels are dry but not brittle. Allow to cool. Store in airtight containers in a cool place, or freeze. As with drying fruit, this process condenses the natural sweetness of the corn. Add it to stews and soups, to cornbread, and to casserole dishes for a sweet corn taste.

Venison Jerky

½ cup soy sauce
¼ cup Worcestershire sauce
1 teaspoon black pepper
1 teaspoon garlic powder
1 pound venison (hindquarter if possible), partially frozen

For the marinade, mix together soy sauce, Worcestershire sauce, black pepper, and garlic powder. Slice venison with the grain of the meat into ⅓-inch-thick strips. Put venison in a large pan and cover with marinade. Let soak overnight, rotating meat at least once. Line bottom of oven with foil. Heat oven to 200°F. Place meat on oven racks and cook 4 hours. Turn over and cook another 4 hours. Meat needs to be firm to the touch. Remove from oven and let cool completely. Store in airtight containers in a cool place.

Bibliography

2002 Healthy Menominee Long Ago & Today. Green Bay: NAES College and University of Wisconsin Extension, 2002.

Beck, David. *Siege and Survival: History of the Menominee Indians, 1634–1856*. Lincoln: University of Nebraska Press, 2002.

Besaw, Alexander. *Green Bay Gazette*, 16 June 1928. Reprinted in *Wisconsin Indigenous News*. Lawrence: Mammoth Publications, 2011.

Bloomfield, Leonard. *Menominee Texts*. New York: G. E. Stechert, 1928.

Brown, Dorothy Moulding. "Wisconsin Indian Corn Origin Myths." *Wisconsin Archeologist* 21 (1940): 19–27.

Densmore, Frances. *Menominee Music*. Washington, DC: Smithsonian Institution, Bureau of American Ethnology Bulletin 102, 1932.

Dillett, Charles B. "Tribal Legends of the Menominee Indians: How Manabus, a Menominee Jonah, Slew Misinimak, the Giant Fish." *Milwaukee Journal*, 30 March 1930.

Erdrich, Heid. *Original Local: Indigenous Foods, Stories, and Recipes from the Upper Midwest*. St. Paul: Minnesota Historical Society Press, 2013.

Frechette, James. "Origin Story." *Menominee Clans Stories*. University of Wisconsin–Stevens Point. http://www4.uwsp.edu/museum/menominee Clans/origin/.

Gortner, Mrs. John. *Buckeye Cookery and Practical Housekeeping: Compiled from Original Recipes, 1877*. Harvard University/Harvard-Google project. https://archive.org/details/buckeyecookerya00wilcgoog.

Hoffman, W. J. "Mythology of the Menomini Indians." *American Anthropologist* 3, no. 3 (1890): 243–258.

Indian Cook Book. Keshena, WI: Menominee County Womans Club, 1970.

Kaquatosh, Raymond C. *Little Hawk and the Lone Wolf: A Memoir*. Madison: Wisconsin Historical Society Press, 2014.

Kearney, Luke Sylvester. "Lake Shore." *The Hodag and Other Tales of the Logging Camps*. Madison, WI: Madison Democrat Printing Co., 1928.

Keesing, Felix M. *The Menominee Indians of Wisconsin*. 1939. Reprint. New York: Johnson Reprint Corp., 1972.

Marquette, Father Jacques. "The Mississippi Voyage of Jolliet and Marquette, 1673," p. 230. Wisconsin Historical Society, American Journeys Collection. http://content.wisconsinhistory.org/cdm/ref/collection/aj/id /3103.

Norick, Sylvester, OFM. *Outdoor Life in the Menominee Forest*. Chicago: Franciscan Herald Press, 1980.

Skinner, Alanson B. *Material Culture of the Menomini*. New York: Museum of the American Indian, Heye Foundation, 1921.

Skinner, Alanson B., and John Satterlee. "Folklore of the Menomini Indians." *Anthropological Papers of the American Museum of Natural History* 13 (1915): 217–542.

Spindler, George D. *Sociocultural and Psychological Processes in Menomini Acculturation*. University of California Publications in Culture and Society 5. Berkeley: University of California Press, 1955.

Spindler, Louise S. "Menomini Women and Culture Change." *American Anthropological Association* 64, no. 1, part 2 (Feb. 1962): 1–112. Memoir 91.

Tribal Cooking: Traditional Stories and Favorite Recipes. Minwanjigewin Nutrition Project, Great Lakes Inter-Tribal Council. Audubon, IA: Jumbo Jack's Cookbooks, 1996.

Wayaka, Rose. "Menominee Gardens Provide Link to Cultural Past." *2002 Healthy Menominee Long Ago & Today*. Green Bay: NAES College and University of Wisconsin Extension, 2002.

Wescott, Earl Sr. Radio interview. Published in *2002 Healthy Menominee Long Ago & Today*. Green Bay: NAES College and University of Wisconsin Extension, 2002.

Index

Note: Locations are in Wisconsin unless otherwise noted.

About the Author

Thomas Pecore Weso is an enrolled member of the Menominee Indian Nation of Wisconsin. He is the author of many articles, personal essays, and a biography of Langston Hughes with coauthor Denise Low. Weso has a master's degree in Indigenous Studies from the University of Kansas  and teaches at Kansas City Kansas Community College. He is a speaker for the Kansas Humanities Council library program Talk about Literature in Kansas and copublisher of Mammoth Publications. He is also an artist, with paintings in collections throughout the Kansas City area, and he has had solo and group shows at the Haskell Cultural Center, the Hutchinson Arts Center, and other venues.

MARCIA EPSTEIN